THE
Prosperity
Principles

THE
Prosperity
Principles

How to Think & Act
Like a Millionaire

JOEL FOTINOS

Cover and text design by Kathryn Sky-Peck
Cover photograph © iStock.com
Typeset in ITC Berkeley Oldstyle

Hampton Roads Publishing Company, Inc.
Charlottesville, VA 22906
Distributed by Red Wheel/Weiser, LLC
www.redwheelweiser.com

Sign up for our newsletter and special offers by going to
www.redwheelweiser.com/newsletter.

ISBN: 978-1-64297-011-1
Library of Congress Cataloging-in-Publication Data available upon request.

Printed in the United States of America
IBI
10 9 8 7 6 5 4 3 2 1

To Alan and Raphi,
who make my life richer in every way

Contents

PROSPERITY PRINCIPLE THREE, 63

Decide You Will Go the Distance

PART TWO

Act Like a Millionaire

PROSPERITY PRINCIPLE FOUR, 79

Begin Now, Not Later

PROSPERITY PRINCIPLE FIVE, 103

Take Steps Every Single Day

PROSPERITY PRINCIPLE SIX, 133

Mastery

AFTERWORD, 153

Beyond Millions

APPENDIX A, 157

University of Success

APPENDIX B, 161

Success Quotes

APPENDIX C, 169

List of Exercises

There are always many people who help to make a book happen. Many of those who work the hardest are at the publishing company. So I want to give a big "thank you" to Greg Brandenburgh, Christine LeBlond, and *everyone* at Hampton Roads. Thank you also to my family for their support in creating this book. And a big thank you to my teachers along the way for the education and inspiration.

This is a book
to help you acquire
the mindset to riches.

INTRODUCTION

Isn't It Time?

This is not a book about money. It's not a book about finances, where to invest, or how to beat the stock market. There are many books that deal with these topics, but this isn't one of them. This book could be more important than any of those books.

This is a book to help you acquire a mindset of riches. It's about creating a way of living where you aren't controlled by fear, inertia, or poverty. Instead, you are motivated by creative, positive action, and an open mind that is ready to receive. After all, what good is wealth if you don't believe you can achieve it?

According to research I've done over the years, as well as my experience and the experience of those I know, self-made millionaires think and act in certain ways that maximize their ability to both create and receive prosperity.

Thinking and Acting Like a Millionaire

Self-made millionaires think and act in certain ways. I've found that self-made millionaires:

- Are positive.

- Are curious.

- Use their imaginations.

- Have a never-quit mentality.

- Turn their defeats, failures, and weaknesses into strengths.

- Make quick decisions (but are willing to change their mind if need be).

- Believe they can do it, whatever "it" is.

- Are engaged in their lives.

- Are consistent with their actions.

- Act with persistence when things get difficult or they feel bogged down.

- Do everything with passion.

- Are flexible when they need to be and firm when they need to be.

- Are focused on their goals.

- **Ask for help when they need it**

- **Create meaningful rewards along their journey**

- **Work hard and play hard**

That doesn't mean that every self-made millionaire is a master at each one of those things. It does mean, however, that they tend to value those qualities and learn to develop them in their own lives. **You can do this, too.**

This book is inspired by great prosperity teachings from classic bestsellers, most of them written about a hundred years ago. But it's informed by experiences—mine and those of people I've worked with for years now. It's the book I wished I had had many years ago; it would have saved me a lot of time, trouble, and years of struggle.

If Your Life Story Were a Book

Since I work in the publishing industry, indulge me a moment. Let's think of your life using the metaphor of a book. If your life were a book, you would keep writing new chapters in the book of your own life. Each year, each experience would create a new chapter in your life story.

Interestingly enough, many of us are not very good authors. In fact, **some of us are not authors at all; we let other people in our lives, or the circumstances of our lives, create the content of our lives.** In these situations, we become passive, taking a back seat while other people take over and tell us what our life story should be. Can you relate to that? At one point in my own life, I was in a dark place and couldn't even see how I could participate in creating my own story; I felt that I was just somehow a character of some story that someone, or fate, had written for me.

And what's more, **some of us are not even main characters in our own life story.** While the title of your life should be *The Story of YOU,* it often really is *The Story of Everyone Else Who Is More Important Than I Am.* Family members—especially parents—tend to want to write the content of our lives, telling us what to do, what we should and shouldn't want for ourselves, and how we should act.

Another way this is true for us is that we can often spend so much time comparing ourselves to others that we aren't truly ourselves. Instead, we base our decisions and actions and self-worth on how they measure against others.

Think about the story of your life so far. Is it fascinating? Is it prosperous? Or are you somehow stuck in a narrative that seems to go on and on and yet goes nowhere. No plot. Just day after day of the same old same old. Weeks are roughly the same as the week before, months are like the months before, and each year is roughly the same year that we have been living over and over again.

This Book Is Focused on Creating Your Prosperous Future

Whether it's making millions, living in a beautiful home, driving the car(s) of your choice, having a healthy savings account and full financial portfolio, or whatever way you define success (and we'll be looking at that in more detail later on), this book can help you achieve it. Wherever you are starting from, it's meant to be a guide to help you get to more of what you want—and less of what you don't want as well. If you are currently in a comfortable place but want to go from comfortable to wealthy, then the principles in this book can help you.

Or if you are like I was at one time, struggling and in debt, then **The Prosperity Principles can be like a lifeline to give you the help you need to believe in yourself and create the future you want.**

More Than Riches

While this book is aimed at creating more financial wealth, **The Prosperity Principles can be used to create more of anything you**

want. This is an important point: your goal might be to make more money and become a millionaire, but the principles will also work to help you on your journey to create more love in your life, more joy, more peace, more health, more adventure, more anything. The principles are framed for money, simply because it seems like money is often what people focus on as the main thing missing from their lives. So use this book to create a more prosperous life . . . and use this book to create more in any area of your life!

Regardless of where you are starting from, your next chapter can be more abundant than your previous chapter. Your future can be richer than your past.

Your Turning Point

Every person I admire has lived a life filled with ups and downs. It seems like the lives of most people who achieve greatness follow a pattern: they begin in a place that is painful, or difficult, or challenging, or filled with lack and limitation of some sort. And then there is a turning point. This turning point becomes the moment they draw the line in the sand, step over the line, and never look back. From that moment on, everything changes. **They are no longer the victim of their circumstances; they are the author of their future.**

My guess is that this is the point you are at now: the turning point.

What you do from this moment on matters. Every thought and action matter. Everything you do either becomes a way to stay where you are or to move forward. Which do you want? More of the same? Or something more?

Take a moment to really take this in. Reread the paragraph above, maybe even read it out loud if you can. And then take a breath, and answer this question: Do you want more of the same, or something more?

> # What you do from this moment on matters.

We Get What We Settle For

One of the uncomfortable truths about life is this: **we don't always get what we want; we get what we settle for.** After all, if you didn't settle for something, you would get more, right? That's common sense, and yet it's not always something we want to hear. It's uncomfortable because it puts the responsibility of your life squarely on the shoulders of . . . you.

"What do you mean, I've settled for all of this debt? Aren't you just blaming the victim here?" you might be asking. Well, I used to think thoughts like that, too. What do you mean that I settled for this credit card debt? What do you mean that I've settled for this low-paying job? I felt like all of my life was pressing down on me and that I didn't have much choice in what was happening.

And yet . . .

Something inside me realized that if I wasn't the one settling for these outcomes, then why did it feel like I was taking a back seat in my own life? Why did it feel like I was not in control of my life? Why did it feel like I was always waiting and waiting for things to change, and yet nothing ever did?

Your prosperous future is waiting for you. I didn't always believe that when I couldn't "see" the future or how what I wanted would come to me. This book shows the way that I "wrote" the next chapter of my life, from scarcity to wealth. And in these pages, I'll teach you how to do it for yourself.

Argue Your Limitations and They Are Yours

Richard Bach wrote a profound truth in his book *Illusions: The Adventures of a Reluctant Messiah*. There are a number of profound ideas that book, but one in particular was like an arrow that hit the bullseye in my mind when I read it the first time. He wrote, **"Argue your limitations, and sure enough, they're yours."** That idea changed my life.

It's so much easier to blame our circumstances on other people, on other factors, on all the hurdles we have to jump over. Some of those things we label as limitations are very real—I'm not making light of them. Some of the conditions in our life *are* difficult and are not all of our own making. However, **our experience of the conditions in our life is mostly under our control.**

For every reason you can pinpoint as the main reason that you aren't where you want to be, or why haven't achieved what you want to, you can find someone who has had that same reason and yet has had amazing success. There are people who started with even less, people who have more dire circumstances, people who have started out far worse than where you are, and yet they have achieved more.

Just do an internet search for "people who achieved unlikely success" and you'll see amazing stories of people who have done amazing things. If you think age is your limitation, search for amazing people over fifty (or sixty or seventy or eighty, or whatever age), and you will find dozens and dozens of stories of people older than you who started a new chapter in their lives and had great success. Or if you think you're too young, search for amazing people under twenty-five (or twenty, or seventeen, or fifteen, or even twelve) to find stories of people who have achieved amazing things at a young age. Whatever your circumstance, the internet is a great place to find inspiration from others who have shared that same circumstance and overcame it.

Those people didn't settle for mediocrity. Neither should you.

> The more we tell ourselves and anyone who we can get to listen all of the reasons we aren't where we think we should be—financially or in any area of our life—the more those reasons hold us back.

The people who aren't held back are the people who won't be held back by anything.

Which kind of person do you want to be?

Where Did the Prosperity Principles Come From?

I didn't invent the Prosperity Principles, I discovered them by reading the ideas in various books I read over the years by great prosperity teachers like Napoleon Hill, U.S. Andersen, Dr. Joseph Murphy, Ralph Waldo Trine, Ernest Holmes, Wallace Wattles, Helen Wilmans, Annie Rix Militz, Catherine Ponder, Emmet Fox, Eric Butterworth, Florence Scovel Shinn, Thomas Troward, Emma Curtis Hopkins, Anthony Norvell, Christian Larsen, Raymond Charles Barker, James Allen, and many others. They didn't invent the Prosperity Principles eiether, but each one of them discovered them for themselves and taught them in the way they understood them.

I discovered them as more than just "principles" when I began to apply them to my own life. I took certain ideas, adapted them, reworded them so I could understand them better, and created my own process of using them. Sometimes it was easy to apply the ideas to my life, sometimes it was difficult, but always it was beneficial. I learned them in even more profound ways when I taught them to others. Now, more than thirty years later, the Prosperity Principles have become a way of life, and I continue to learn how to apply them in ever deeper ways.

This book brings all of these ideas together in the most succinct, easy-to-use ways.

My History with Money

In many ways, I'm the least likely person to write this book. Raised in a small town in Nebraska, my family was never flush with cash. My parents, while intelligent, weren't graduates from Ivy League schools, and had no special connections or "family money." They were hardworking people who often worked multiple jobs to pay the bills and allow us to have fun as well. It was a frequent sight to see overdrafts in our mailbox—those pink slips that required my parents to pay an extra $20 fee for every check that bounced. At least one or two of those pink overdraft slips seemed to make it into our mailbox each month. I'm not suggesting we were living hand-to-mouth, but we definitely weren't affluent. There were many nights my parents stayed awake trying to figure out how they were going to pay all of their bills.

Living in that small town in Nebraska didn't seem to offer many opportunities to increase our financial standing. At age nine I began working in the grocery store my father owned—cleaning, stocking the shelves, bagging groceries for customers, and even occasionally as cashier. When the business closed, my parents needed cash for our move to another town, and we kids contributed our earnings to the move. Starting over again wasn't unknown to us.

Throughout my childhood (and even when I was older), my mother often worked three jobs at a time. When I was thirteen, my father arranged to have me begin working at a friend's restaurant (for $1.65/hour, no tips). When I turned fourteen, I added a second job at the town's bookstore, and then at sixteen I added a third job working at one of the local shoe stores. I also had two paper routes (the local paper and the big *Omaha World-Herald*) and took various other odd jobs that came up (mowing lawns, tele-sales for the local policeman's ball, etc.). I took some courses at the local college and then moved to Denver, the nearest big city. At eighteen I became assistant manager, and then manager for a chain bookstore in one of the local shopping malls. In addition to my full-time job, I did various jobs on my days off, since I was always broke. Like my parents before me, I developed the habit of being overdrawn frequently and working as many jobs as possible to pay for my bills.

The story of my life seemed small, and it was about to take a turn for the worse.

23 CREDIT CARDS

I had developed another bad habit during these years, one I created all by myself . . . using credit cards to pay for everything.

Eventually my credit card habit grew into an addiction. The credit card companies kept sending me cards in the mail, all with "special offers," and I took advantage of every one of them. I figured, if the credit card company thinks I can afford yet another card, who am I to argue? Well, of course, I learned the hard way. The more credit cards I used, the more in debt I became. The more in debt I became, the more I learned how dark and oppressive the world of debt can be. Eventually I got to the point of having twenty-three active credit cards, and nearly $60,000 in personal credit card debt. My salary at the time was half that amount, and I was living just north of San Francisco, where the cost of living is very high.

With basic living expenses, plus twenty-three minimum payments to make each month, I was essentially just moving credit card balances around to try to stay afloat. Eventually I reached a breaking point (which I describe in more detail in my book *My Life Contract*) and finally began the journey from debt to debt-free and then to prosperity.

When I was at my lowest, I thought that what I needed to go from overwhelming debt to becoming debt-free was just a check for the amount of debt I was in. But what I learned on the journey to becoming debt-free was that in order for me to receive more prosperity in life, first I had to *become* more in life. **I had to learn how to *be* a different person in order to have a different experience.** To be completely candid, learning how to be a different person was the last thing I wanted. I wanted the easy and quick way out, just something to erase the debt. But I committed myself to the journey, and now, looking back, I can see that the easy way out wouldn't have changed me, it would only have temporarily changed my bank account. If my mind and actions didn't change, then my outcome wouldn't change. If I didn't learn the principles of true prosperity and change my life, I would have no doubt gotten back into debt, and probably even worse. There are studies that show that people who win the lottery more often than not experience a brief respite from their monetary woes, but then get into more financial trouble than before they won the lottery. Why? Because they didn't expand their personal definitions and change their actions. They didn't write a new story for themselves.

There are certain qualities and principles of prosperity that I needed to learn before I could actually experience lasting prosperity in my life. I needed to acquire a "Millionaire Mindset" before actually becoming a millionaire. Lasting change needs to come from within, and as I did the work to make those changes in both my mindset and in my actions, my external experience changed as well. That's what we're learning in this book.

Remember those twenty-three credit cards and the nearly $60,000 in debt? Well, long story short, on the day that I decided I couldn't live the way I had been and committed to change, I decided that the first thing I should do was to see an accountant for a professional opinion of my situation. I went to his office (well, it was actually a cubicle; he worked in a large firm). He took all my bills and my information (salary, monthly rent, etc.) and used an old-fashioned calculator to run all the numbers. At last, when he was done, he looked at all the papers from his calculations, looked up at me, and said, "Good news! If you don't use your credit cards again, and if your salary increases at a reliable rate over the years, it will only take you twenty-eight years to get out of debt!" Twenty-eight years! And then he gave me his bill, which of course I paid with my credit card. I was definitely in a dark place, financially and emotionally. Maybe you can relate to this in some way? If so, keep reading, there is good news ahead.

Write the Next Chapter

Here's how that chapter of my story ended: I did dig myself out of debt, but instead of taking twenty-eight years, I did it in just over three and a half years. And along the way, my salary contin-ued to grow, taking some major jumps. My savings accounts grew, and eventually I went from having not enough, to "just enough," to more than enough. I began teaching these ideas to others and seeing their lives change for the better as well. Regardless of their situation, the ideas helped them realize positive results. You'll read the stories of some of these people throughout the book.

I learned how to write my next chapter and become the hero of my own story. I'll teach you how I did it in these pages. Let me say this again: **If I can do this, you can, too. Really.**

My hope is that you will be inspired by my story, and the stories of others, to write a whole new chapter of your life story.

What Does "More" Mean to You?

The definition of "more" is different for each one of us. One thing I have learned is that my definition changed over the years as I changed. My "more" grew and changed as I grew and changed.

One of the books that has had a powerful impact on me is *Think and Grow Rich* by Napoleon Hill. When I first saw the book, my focus was mainly on the word "rich." As I began to read it, I began to think that the important word was actually "think"— how to consider my way to wealth. If I thought in a certain way, I would have money galore. But by the time I had reread the book several times, I realized that the most important word in the title is actually "grow." Hill writes over and over that there is no such thing as something for nothing. We can't expect to receive more while we remain exactly the same. **In order to have more, we must first become more. As we grow, our circumstances grow, including our finances.**

However you define "more" in your life, hold on to it loosely, and let yourself continue to evolve and redefine success.

What Do You Need to Do?

My hope is that you will read through this book with an open mind. I know that there is a tendency to find ways to say "Well, that couldn't happen to me . . ." But while the exact experiences will be different for every person, the Prosperity Principles are time-honored and have worked for millions of self-made millionaires over the years. I didn't invent these principles, I discovered them and then applied them to my situation. That's my wish for you: that you read this book, take away the positive ideas in each chapter, and then find ways to apply these ideas to your own situation.

Now, here's a hard truth, and I'm going to just come out and tell it to you. If you are not where you want to be financially (and actually, in any area of your life), then you need to know this:

> If you do not change your attitude and your actions for the better, then your situation will not change for the bettter.

I know that sounds obvious, but one thing I have found from my own experience, and from having taught these ideas to thousands of people over the years, is this: we often say we want change, but we don't commit to the change. Then nothing changes, and then we complain about it. It's important for you to embrace this simple truth—you *will* need to change your attitude, and you *will* need to change your actions.

How This Book Is Organized

This book has several parts. I want you to read it, but more importantly I want you to use the ideas and actions as tools for your transformation. You can use them to write your next chapter and grow rich in the ways that you want.

The book itself is divided into two parts: **Think Like a Millionaire** and **Act Like a Millionaire.** The chapters in the first part are focused on changing and enlarging your mindset to create the wealth that you wish to have. Part One is about adopting the mind of a millionaire. Those in the second part are focused on the positive million-dollar actions you can take that will support you as you create your new chapter.

Throughout the book there are small sections that serve as powerful reminders of the ideas you just read about. Sections called DO THIS include actions to take to move you forward. While they are suggestions, I strongly encourage you to practice them, not just read them. To paraphrase the 13th-century Sufi poet Rumi, you can't get drunk on just the word 'wine.' He meant that you need to drink the wine in order to feel its effects. Similarly, you need to "do" the book to experience it.

Each chapter concludes with a STOP and START section. These are pretty self-explanatory. STOP includes ideas of what to cease doing as these activities will hamper you on your journey. START includes ideas of what to begin doing to aid you on your journey.

Finally, there are two things I encourage you to do as you read the book, to maximize your experience of thinking and acting like a millionaire:

Journal—Get a journal to write your thoughts, goals, and actions and to chart your progress. As you write a new chapter in your life, literally write about it! I will refer to writing in your journal occasionally throughout the book. Believe me, your journal will become a valued companion on your journey to riches.

Success Partner—Find someone to read and "do" this book with. Pick a best friend, significant other, trusted coworker, or family member. Make sure to pick someone who is as dedicated as you are, who will support you as much as you support them, and who you will be accountable to, so that you both take this endeavor more seriously.

I was once talking to a friend when I discovered that we both had the same financial goal, which was to become a millionaire. We decided to meet regularly to talk through our journey and to make the other person accountable for our actions. We even named our partnership the Million Dollar Club, and when we met, we focused on our goal and what we were doing to accomplish it. It was great to have a companion on the road to riches. We helped each other by seeing the "millionaire" in each other before we could even see it for ourselves.

Meet with your success partner regularly, discuss the ideas in the book and how they apply to your life situations, and then do the activities together. Bring your journals and make each meeting focused on your goals (no complaining allowed!).

Speaking of no complaining, try to not complain or speak negatively—about a situation, about other people, or about yourself. A self-help author once said, "Your word is your wand," meaning that the words you say—externally or internally—help to create the experience you have. So it's vitally important to use your words wisely, both the ones you say out loud and those you say to yourself. Develop the habit of positive talk and positive self-talk.

When you are tempted to complain about something, ask yourself these questions:

- **Is what you are complaining about something you can change or affect? If so, then do something about it. Then you don't need to complain.**

- Is what you are complaining about something you cannot change or affect? If so, then complaining about it is a waste of energy. Stop.

One More Thing, One More Thing, One More Thing

Let me confess something right here. I do repeat certain ideas several times, and I do that by design. It's because those ideas are important enough to be repeated so that they make an impression.

Okay, it's time. Open your mind, get ready to take some positive actions to experience prosperity in your life, and turn the page.

Part
One

Think Like a Millionaire

In order to go somewhere,
first we must know
where we are starting.

Be Clear about Your Starting Point

The story of your life is made up of the experiences you've had and the people you've known up to this moment. At every moment you have the ability to either continue the story in the direction it has been or to steer it in an entirely new direction, including this moment right now.

It's important, as we begin this journey together, to know that every journey begins with a starting point. That is where you are right now. By "where" I mean, where in your life you are, in *every* area of your life. How happy are you? How happy are you with your finances? Your career? Your relationships? Your general well-being?

In order to go somewhere, first you must know where you're starting from. If you were to go on a journey using the GPS function on your smartphone, you would need both the starting point and the ending point to get the directions. It's the same with the story of your life. Let's begin by getting clear about where you are as you write this new chapter. It's the first step in creating your new prosperous story.

Frame Your Story

When you think about the story you tell about your life, how do you tell it? What people or experiences do you focus on? Do you characterize your life as a triumph? Or a tragedy? Or do you flippantly say, "The story of my life would make people go to sleep!" You might feel that you haven't accomplished what you wanted to, or that you're stuck, or that you have many hopes and dreams. How you tell your story—to yourself and to others—matters.

It's interesting to note that the same set of experiences can be described in different ways. If ten people go to the same movie, and you ask them all to describe what the movie was about, you would most likely get ten different versions. One movie, ten different ways of seeing it.

We have the same ability to tell and retell the story of our life in different ways.

This is important because I want you to begin a new chapter of your life story, and how you tell this new story is influenced by the story you have already been telling.

Have you ever met someone new and very quickly they begin to tell you all their troubles and problems? How does that feel when that happens? Do you feel a bit trapped by them? Or do you join in and start talking about all your troubles and problems? If you start out talking to someone this way, you frame life through the lens of your troubles and problems.

We can also frame our lives through our triumphs and successes. We don't have to be boastful or arrogant about it, but we can see our life as one of overcoming adversity rather than being overcome.

Whichever way you have framed your life up to now, take a moment to reflect on whether you are a person who concentrates more on the positive or on the negative. Are you someone who tells a story of your joys or of your trials?

Here's a powerful exercise that can help reveal many things about your life to you. It's something that had a profound impact on me and helped me to reframe not only my past, but how I view my future.

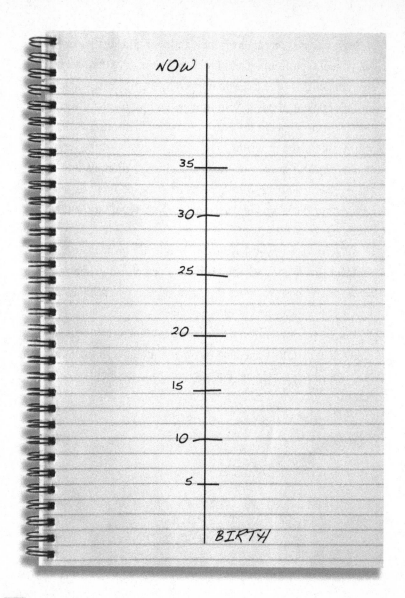

NOW

35

30

25

20

15

10

5

BIRTH

THE PROSPERITY PRINCIPLES

☞ DO THIS:
Create Your Timeline

In your journal (or on a sheet of paper), draw a line down the center. At the bottom of the line, write the word "birth" and at the top of the line right "now." Put ticks along the line to denote periods of time (age five, ten, fifteen, etc., or any other denotation). It looks something like the example on page 28.

Now, take a few moments and begin thinking about the important experiences that have shaped your life. These can include things like: graduating from grade/middle/high school or college, first job, getting married, etc. It can include significant health challenges you faced (surgeries or major illnesses), relationship points (met significant other, got married/divorced, broke up), changed jobs, bought a house, and more. You can make this as detailed (or not) as you want. Now add significant experiences you've had. Add anything else that seems important, such as traveled to someplace significant, when a loved one died, or you discovered a new hobby that became a lifelong passion.

But I want you to add those things on your timeline in a particular way. If the experience was negative, chart it on one side of the line (I used the left side for this), and if the experience was positive or neutral, chart it on the other side of the line (I used the right side for this). A very simplified version could look like the example on page 30.

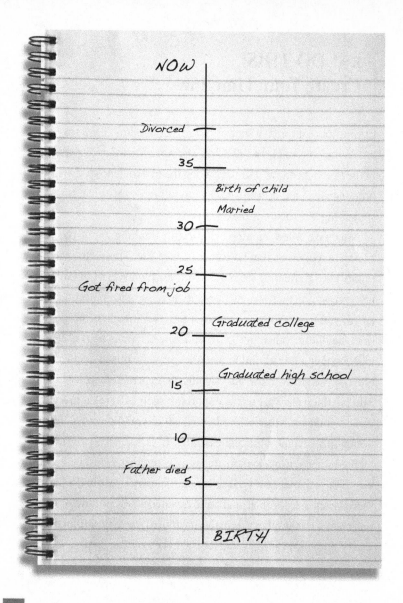

THE PROSPERITY PRINCIPLES

NOTE – You can alter this exercise in any way that adds meaning to you. The point is to create a map that gives you a snapshot of some of the highs and lows.

When I did this exercise, it had a profound effect on me. First, I noticed how many positive experiences I filled in. So much of what I dwelled on were the negative experiences that I often forgot to remember that my life had many positive experiences as well.

Second, I noticed something unexpected, which is that many of the most significantly positive experiences that I had happened shortly after some of the most negatives ones. In some cases, the negative experiences seemed to usher in something positive. A negative would seemingly result in a positive later on. Consciously or subconsciously, I somehow turned my setbacks into positive experiences.

And third, this timeline game me a sense of how much life I had lived. It gave me appreciation for all I've come through and compassion for myself. Like many people, I was often so hard on myself in the privacy of my own mind, berating myself for not being enough, for being too different, for my lack of a good job or money in the bank, for being overweight, etc. But seeing how much I went through to get to that point, I was filled with a sense of gratitude for my younger self and how brave I had been to get to where I was, even if it wasn't yet where I wanted to be.

I've since done this exercise with many people in workshops and classes, and I've seen firsthand how this simple exercise can create some profound revelations.

This exercise helps to create the Millionaire Mind.

It isn't for navel-gazing. It gives you a sense of your origins and also your patterns, your strengths, and those areas where you might need some help. **Self-knowledge helps to build prosperity.**

This exercise also gives you a history you can draw from as you write this new chapter of your life. The best books I've read—whether they are memoirs or novels—always give the reader a sense of the history of each character. The more a reader knows the backstory of a character, the richer the reading experience and the greater the sense of how much the character had to overcome.

For my timeline, on the left side, I put "got into $60,000 in credit card debt," but on the right side I put "became debt free." That doesn't tell the whole story of course, but it frames an important part of it.

As you look at your timeline, do you see any patterns? That brings us to an important point to remember . . .

Patterns

Many people keep creating the same experience over and over again. This can range from deep-seated patterns, learned in our childhoods, to habits that we've acquired over the years.

When I was a kid, my mother often said:

"If you always do what you always did, you'll always get what you always got."

She would tell me this to try to get me to make better choices, usually around school or the house. But this simple little saying is actually an important lesson for all of us.

The level of your success at this point in your life is the sum of your thoughts, beliefs, and actions up to now. And if you keep living your life with the same thoughts, beliefs, and actions, then you'll continue to achieve roughly the same amount of success. **You won't get something different until you *do* something different. And you won't do different things until you *become* different.**

There is a business saying that is similar to what my mother used to say. It goes like this: **what brought you here won't take you there.** And the great New Thought teacher Wallace Wattles said that **you can't have more until you first become more** (that's my paraphrase, by the way). All of this is to say that once you truly know who you are—warts and all—then you can move forward.

The Line in the Sand

So let this be the line in the sand, this moment, right now. I'm
going to draw a line here for you:

**THIS
MOMENT**

WHO I WAS   **WHO I AM
BECOMING**

A little further in the book I'm going to ask you to make your final decision to live your life your new way: to release limiting thoughts and actions and create new, empowering thoughts and habits that will bring you your goal. For now, I want you to look at the line and see if you are ready for the story of your life to take a new, prosperous turn. The following exercise will help you cross that line in the sand.

Are you ready for MORE?

☞ DO THIS: Let Go of What You Don't Want

For this exercise, you'll use the line above or draw one in your journal. On one side of the line I want you to write "who I was" and list all the things you don't want to bring with you in your new chapter of wealth. Some of the things you might write include: debt, negative people (by name), procrastination, clutter, a job I don't like, etc. These are not things you will necessarily shed immediately, but they are things you are willing to let go of once you cross the line. They belong in your old life, not where you are headed.

On the other side of the line, write "who I am" and list the opposite of each thing that you already wrote. If you wrote "credit card debt" on the side "who I was" then on the other side of the line write "debt free." Do this with each thing you wrote. Through this action, you are creating a mental image of what you want, rather than focusing on what you don't. You are writing what you want to experience.

☞ DO THIS: Create a Cast of Characters

In your journal, write a list of the people who are actively in your life. These are the people you live with, work with, hang around with. These might be friends, coworkers, family members, and anyone else who is a constant presence in your life.

This is your cast of characters. These are the people you are surrounded by. As in a novel, some of them may be heroes, some of them might be villains, many of them might be supporting players.

Look at the list and note which of the people on the list are positive influences, who fill you with energy when you are with them. Which of the people on the list are negative influences, who drain you of energy when you are with them (or even when you think about them)? Which ones are neutral? For now, just notice. Are the majority of the people in your life positive influences? Or are most of them negative? Or a mix of both?

☞ DO THIS:
Release the Past

Before we begin creating the life you want, take a moment to release and let go of your past. Take a few minutes to look at both the timeline you created and the cast of characters. Some of what you wrote fills you with joy and empowerment, some of what you wrote might make you angry or sad, and some of it just is what it is. In any case, the total of all of what you wrote is what brought you to this moment.

Now, in your mind (or you can write this out in your journal), say "thank you" to everything that brought you here—the positive, the negative, everything. You aren't condoning negative things, and you aren't brushing over hardships. Instead, you are acknowledging that through it all, you are still here and you are now getting ready to let go and move on to greater experiences. Acknowledge all of your experiences, thank them, and then mentally release them. You can say to yourself (or write in your journal), "I now release the past and embrace the future." Or anything else that will conclude this chapter of your life.

Now, take a breath and imagine yourself turning the page. A new, greater, more prosperous chapter is about to begin.

Use the following powerful reminders as you continue on your journey to prosperity. You can turn them into affirmations or post them where you'll see them often.

Stop:

- Thinking that your goals and wants are in some ambiguous "someday."

- Holding on to the past, or thinking that the past can hold you back.

- Thinking that you aren't the type of person who can have success.

- Complaining about anything or anyone.

- Practicing negative habits or actions.

Start:

- Realizing that your goals are your responsibility and that you can start achieving them now.

- Forming new, positive habits.

- Affirming over and over "I release the past and embrace the future" and "I deserve success."

- Talking about yourself in positive ways.

Riches
do not respond
to wishes.

Be Clear about Where You Want to Go

We began the last chapter by beginning to get clear about where we are starting from. Now it's time to set some goals. You picked up this book with some sense of what you want to create— more success, more money, greater financial experience. Now it's time to get specific.

What Do You Want?

Napoleon Hill, author of *Think and Grow Rich*, wrote something in that book, originally published in 1937, that still is true today: most people cannot tell you exactly what they want and how they are going to get it. He wrote,

Examine the first hundred people you meet, ask them what they want most in life, and ninety-eight of them will not be able to tell you. If you press them for an answer, some will say security, many will say money, a few will say happiness, others will say fame and power, and still others will say social recognition, ease in living, ability to sing, dance, or write, but none of them will be able to define these terms, or give the slightest indication of a plan by which they hope to attain these vaguely expressed wishes. Riches do not respond to wishes. They respond only to definite plans, backed by definite desires, through constant persistence.

Out of one hundred people, ninety-eight couldn't be specific—that's 98 percent. Are you one of the 98 percent? If so, take heart. You are about to become one of the 2 percent of people who know what they want and how they are going to get it.

> # The 2 percent are the ones who think and act like a millionaire.

Setting Goals

There are entire books written about how to set goals—what they are, what you should never do when setting goals, etc. I've spent a lot of time on this topic, trying out different types of goals and goal setting. And here is what I've found: **keep it simple, super simple,** or KISSS. That's a play on the acronym KISS, which stands for Keep It Simple, Stupid. However, I'm not stupid, and neither are you, so I modified it to make it even clearer!

I've noticed, for both myself and for nearly all of the people I've worked with over the years, that the simpler a goal is, the likelier we are to achieve it. Many people set goals that are:

- **Too complicated**

- **Too distant**

- **Too gigantic/unachievable**

- **Too small**

- **Too uninspiring**

- **Too vague**

- **Too much like what other people want for you**

When you set goals that are like any of the above, they will be hard to take from dream to reality. **The clearer and simpler your goals are, the more achievable they are.**

Not Too Big, Not Too Small, Just Right

Let me share a little secret that will help you create a goal: You don't have to make just one goal for your life. Some people get hung up on setting a goal because they think that one goal is what they'll need to work on for the rest of their life. What is better, is to **create a goal that inspires you, delights you, and is just beyond your reach. Then, when you achieve that goal, you can set your next goal, and the next, and so on.** If you do have a huge goal, then you can break it down into smaller goals.

Here's another piece of good news: you can change your goal as you go along. If you find that you've set a goal that is too small or you chose a goal that was something you thought you should choose rather than something inspiring, then change it. You should not need to change your goals that often, but goals can grow and change and expand as you grow and change and expand.

The point of having a goal is to have something that motivates you to achieve it. It's meant to be something that excites you, gets you out of bed in the morning, and keeps you wanting to move toward it. If you choose something that doesn't do those things, then you need to choose better. Napoleon Hill wrote, "Small fires create small heat." This means that if your goal is too weak, then it won't be something you're excited to work toward.

On the other hand, if you choose a goal that is too big, too audacious, then it's going to feel overwhelming to try to achieve it.

> ## Picking a goal that is far too big is a way of self-sabotaging your own success.

Picking something that is far beyond your reach will make it too easy to say to yourself, "See, this goal stuff doesn't work!" It didn't work because you chose something unachievable.

Let me be clear. In one sense, all goals can be achieved. However, if you're deep in debt and you pick "I want one billion dollars" as your goal, that is probably not going to happen. However, if you are deep in debt and choose "I want to be debt free" as your first goal, that is far more achievable, and once you achieve that, you can then create further goals. And then who knows? Maybe you can eventually level up to a billion dollars. But start with something that will work.

Similarly, if you choose a goal that is too small, then it won't inspire you. A person in one of my workshops said his goal was to have a salary of $50,000. I asked what his salary was at the time, and he said it was $45,000. That was a goal of earning $5,000. When I questioned if this was a big enough goal, he assured me it was. He soon dropped out of the class, and when I emailed him to ask why he left, he wrote that the class didn't seem to really inspire him. It wasn't the class that didn't inspire him, it was his goal. If he had chosen an exciting goal, then the class would have served him to achieve it.

> Picking too small a goal is another
> form of self-sabotage.

Tell Me What You Want, What You Really, Really Want

When I ask, "What do you want?"—what is the first thing (or things) that come to mind? If I asked, "What would you love to have in the next six months or year?" Usually there is a quick idea that pops in our mind *before* our inner critic can shame us into choosing something else. Someone might think "to be a millionaire" before our rational mind (thinking it is helping you) rushes in with thoughts like, "That's too much" or "I don't deserve that" or "How could a million dollars ever appear in my life?" Whatever first popped in your head might be something to consider for your goal, or at least a starting place to determine your goal. In the example above, if a million dollars just feels too crazy or unattainable, then adjust it. I want your goal to feel:

- **Inspiring**

- **Desirable**

- **Achievable (without having to know "how")**

- **Next Level**

- **Luxurious**

- **Joyful**

Did you notice that I didn't mention picking a goal that you knew how to achieve? Pick a goal that is just beyond where you can figure out how to achieve, and then you can figure out how to achieve it along the way. The "how" will come step-by-step, and a lot of how will be through people or experiences that you can't even predict! And for goodness' sake, don't choose a goal based on your current salary.

☞ DO THIS: Pick a Goal

It's time to pick a goal. If you need some help, here are some of the most common goals that I've seen people choose over the years:

- **No credit card debt**

- **No mortgage**

- **Savings account (name a specific amount)**

- **Student loan paid off**

- **A million dollars**

- **Multiple streams of income**

- **Great job**

- **Beautiful home**

- **A new car**

- **Travel to (name specific vacation spot or cruise)**

On the line below, or in your journal, write down what goal comes to mind:

_____

Now take a breath.

Again, this doesn't have to be the one and only goal you ever set. It doesn't have to be the greatest goal of all time. This is just meant to be your next goal. You can set many more after you achieve this one.

Look at the goal again. Is it too small? Too big? If you want, go back and cross out what you wrote, and adjust it a bit. If it feels a little too big, that's okay. You want something that is going to stretch you.

But How?

The single most common comment I hear from people in my workshops and classes is that they would love to set a goal that inspires them, but they just don't see how that goal can come to them. Sometimes "how" is the poison in our mind that keeps us from taking chances and choosing greatness.

I'm not suggesting you take reckless risks or believe in something that doesn't make sense. I am, however, asking you to push aside the question of how when creating your goal. Think of people who have achieved things. When they set out to make their goals and dreams come true, they didn't know every single step they would take to materialize it. Instead, they just took steps forward and figured things out along way. As they moved forward, they would experience synchronicities and coincidences, or meet people along the way that helped at them key moments, or things would happen that they never could have imagined. We don't have to know the whole path; we only need to take a step onto the path.

Many years ago, I went to a talk given by a Buddhist monk. This talk was held in a big beautiful home in Colorado, by invitation only (I was invited as the "plus one" of one of my friends). I walked into the house and immediately felt intimidated by the size of it and obvious wealth on display. It was light-years away from my tiny apartment, which I could barely afford at my $9,000/year salary. The people who owned this house had everything, and I felt that I had so little.

As the seventy or so guests chatted with each other in the stunning, spacious living room, I looked around feeling like I didn't belong because I didn't have as much (money, possessions, confidence, etc.) as the others in the room. Part of me wanted to run from the situation and go home. I felt so small.

And then suddenly the conversation ended, and the room became silent. I looked around to see what had changed, and that's when I saw a small man had entered. He was Asian and dressed in an orange robe. He had a small satchel dangling from his waist. As it turns out, everything that this monk owned in the world was in that satchel. I wondered what was in it—a comb? A little package of tissues? Some Altoids?

He made his way to the chair that had been placed at the head of the room and sat down. Everyone came and sat on the floor around him. I had a great seat, pretty near him on his left. He gave a Dharma talk, which is like a short, inspirational Buddhist sermon, about how we can choose to be happy and content by making some simple changes. Making simple changes, he said, can have profound and long-lasting effects. He spoke so quietly that we all had to lean in to hear him. While he was talking, I noticed a woman who was sitting on the floor to his right. I noticed her because she was clearly getting more and more agitated as he spoke. She was making loud sighs, shaking her head, and making other distracting gestures. When the monk was done speaking, he asked for questions, and this woman's hand shot up immediately. He nodded to her to ask her question, and she began speaking a mile a minute, waving her hands, at a loud volume. It was a jarring contrast to his slow, measured, and thoughtful manner.

She jumped right in. "I hear you talk about *how* we can be happy and *how* we can be content, and *how* we can choose to make changes and *how* we can achieve nirvana and *how* we can create a different life experience, but I don't see *how* I can do it. *How* can I accomplish these things? *How* am I supposed to make this real for me?" She went on and on.

The monk let her speak, and as she spoke, he looked at her with compassion and silence, not interrupting. When she was done, he took a breath and was silent for a minute. Everyone in the room was like statues, wondering how this gentle monk was going to answer this very agitated person. It was almost as if she just wanted to be heard. I had no idea of how he could answer her questions.

At last, the monk began to speak, again in his slow, quiet way. "Mmmm, very interesting questions . . . how to achieve this. How to do this . . . How to accomplish peace . . . How, how, how . . . So many 'hows' . . . Big questions . . . big hows . . ." He was silent for a few seconds and then said, "Big how . . . the answer is . . . Little how." In that moment, the energy in the room shifted as we all (including the woman who had asked the question) understood what he had said. In four words, he had said as much as some books! Big how? Answer is little how. **Big how, little how.** Replace the word "how" with "goals" and it goes like this: Big goals? The answer is little goals. Now replace the word "how" with dreams: Big dreams? The answer is little dreams.

Don't be intimidated by your goal.

> Whatever your goal is, it can be broken down into smaller goals that lead to the bigger goal.

☞ DO THIS: Expand Your Goal a Bit More

Hopefully at this point you have written down a goal. If you want to adjust it a bit more, now is the time.

Done? Okay, let's move on. We're going to take your goal and polish it a bit.

Look at your goal and answer the following questions. Write your answers down in the space below or in your journal. Don't overthink your answers, just write down whatever comes to your mind first.

- How does this goal make you feel?

- What does this goal mean to you? (In other words, why did you pick this particular goal?)

- Imagine yourself achieving this goal—how does that moment feel?

- How would it feel if you didn't accomplish this goal in the next six months or year?

- What is the first step (or two) that you could take toward accomplishing this goal?

- What needs to change for you to achieve this goal?

- What do you need to stop doing to help reach this goal?

- What do you need to start doing to help reach this goal?

- Who in your life can help you with your goal?

- Who in your life might hinder you from reaching your goal?

- When would you like to achieve this goal?

Good job. Take a moment and review your answers. Have you learned anything?

These questions flesh out your goal so it's not just "I want a million dollars" but the "why" you want it, and the "how it makes you feel" to have it. If you know why you choose a goal and how achieving that goal will make you feel, you will be far more apt to stick with making the goal become real.

☞ DO THIS:
Write Down Your Goals

The great prosperity teachers of the last hundred years have all recommended the practice of writing down your goals. Why? Because there is something that is more "real" about a goal when you write it down. It becomes more concrete. Rather than being something you just talk about it becomes something you are now looking to achieve. On page 55 is a form you can use to write down your goal (or write it your journal).

Congratulations, you have set your first goal. It's the map you'll use to navigate your way from wishful thinking to a millionaire mind.

Read it out loud. How does it feel when you read it?

Make a copy of your goal—you can even use an index card. This card, with your goal written on it, should be placed on your bedside table. Why? Because you are going to **read your goal right when you wake up, and then you are going to read it**

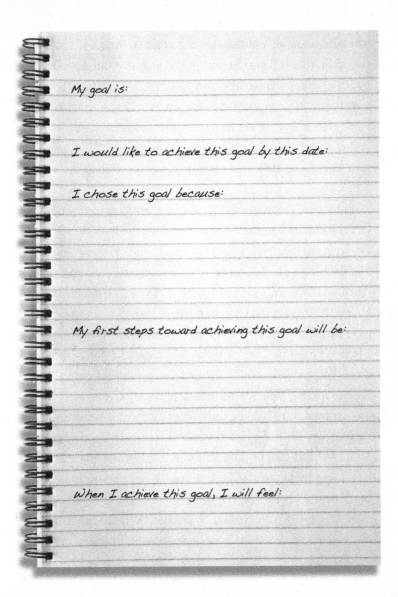

My goal is:

I would like to achieve this goal by this date:

I chose this goal because:

My first steps toward achieving this goal will be:

When I achieve this goal, I will feel:

just before turning out the light out at night. Why am I asking you to do that? I'll answer that question with a question: How might your day change if you began your day and ended it with a reminder of your goal? I'm sure you would agree that book-ending your day by reading your goal (preferably out loud!) will make you more focused on it throughout the day, and in turn that focus will help you get closer to your goal, faster. That's why.

Every time I've taught this in a multi-week class, someone has raised their hand and said something along the lines of "I'm just not seeing as much results as I thought I would at this point . . ." The first question I ask them is "Are you reading your goal right when you wake up and again right before you turn out the lights at night?" And 100 percent of the time, they give me an excuse as to why they haven't been doing this. Common excuses are a) I forget; b) I'm in a hurry in the mornings; c) I don't see how this is going to help; d) I feel stupid saying this goal out loud or even to myself. Here are the quick answers I give when I hear these excuses: a) Place the card right next to your bedside table light or where your eye will see it immediately upon waking. It's a card and it's not difficult to find an obvious place for it. b) It takes about eight seconds to read it. Are you really in that big of hurry? I bet you spend more time looking at social media than this! (This is the lamest of excuses, even though it is really common.) c) You really don't see how starting and ending your day thinking of your highest goal is going to inspire you? Really?! We'll discuss this in more detail later in the book, by the way, and d) It's better to feel a little stupid now and achieve your goal, than to avoid saying it and not achieve your goal. If you have a mental block preventing you from doing this simple exercise, get over it! Just do it. Trust me; do it for thirty days and see if you see any results. Do it for your results, and do it for yourself. And if that doesn't convince you, then just do it for me, pretty please.

☞ DO THIS: Practice Your Elevator Pitch

Remember the quote from Napoleon Hill's book *Think and Grow Rich*, about the 98 percent of people not being able to answer the question, "What do you want?" Well, congratulations, you are now officially among the 2 percent of people who can. Not only do you know the answer, but I've encouraged you to read it every moment upon waking and every evening before lights out.

Now I'm going to ask you to also memorize it. Say it over and over again until you don't need the "script" to read it from. Make it something that you say over and over inside your head—when you're walking down the street, standing in line, or even cleaning, this is going through your head.

There are several reasons for doing this. First, if for some reason someone asks you "What do you want?" you will be able to answer like the most confident person ever. You have practiced your elevator pitch.

Second, and more importantly, what you say to yourself matters. We're going to dig a little deeper into this later in the book, but suffice to say for now, by memorizing your goal and repeating it often, you are feeding your mind positive input, which in turn will help you have a more positive outlook, and that in turn will help you have a more positive experience.

The more committed you are to immersing yourself in your goal, the more you develop your millionaire mind. The more you say your goal, the more you embody it.

Who Do You Tell Your Goal To?

Now that you have a goal, have written it down, and repeat it frequently to yourself throughout the day, you might think that I would tell you share your goal with everyone in your life. Please don't.

Keep your goal to yourself. And then choose to reveal it only to those people who support you, are positive influences, and can help you. Why? Because you have chosen to do something that is going to require you to grow and change. Some of the people in your life have a very specific image of you in their heads and don't want it to change. If you told a negative person about your new goal, they might reply with something like, "You? You never follow through on things. Don't get your hopes up!" Or they might even say worse things.

> **Sometimes the people in your life can only see who you have been, not who you are becoming.**

Choose wisely. It won't feel good to share something so precious as your goal with someone who doesn't value you or support you on your journey to achieving it. The phrase "do not cast your pearls before swine" is another way of saying this. Not that the people in your life are swine, but rather the metaphor is that as you grow and expand in your experience, the people who don't grow and expand can't see the beauty of your goal. Also, some people are jealous and will feel superior to have you not reach your goal. Have you ever met a person like that? I'm sure you have! So steer clear of them, please.

Your New Normal

There is power in your words. You now have very specific words that will bring you more power. Your goal is your gold. It's your map. It's your path toward realizing your dreams. It's your millionaire mind in action!

What you are doing by creating this goal and repeating it often is creating a "new normal." This means that **you are already transforming your life, because you are changing how you speak and being specific and inspired by something that excites you.**

This is exciting.

I'm excited for you.

But before we go further, review the following powerful reminders to help you go the distance:

Stop:

- **Asking others what they think you should do.**

- **Being vague about what you want.**

- **Holding back and accepting less than what you want.**

- **Sharing your goal with those who don't support you.**

Start:

- Choosing the most positive, joyful action or the action that brings you positivity/joy.

- Writing down your goal and reading it every morning and night.

- Memorizing your goal and repeating it often, both in your head and out loud, believing that you will achieve this goal and every goal you set.

**Take your goal
from dream
to reality.**

Decide You Will Go the Distance

You've gotten very clear about your life as it is up to this point. You spent time picking a simple-but-exciting goal and learned not only what goal you chose, but why you chose it and how it will change your life. You've done some of the groundwork needed to go from a limited mind to a millionaire mind.

There is one more vital step to take. And that is to make the decision to go forward. This step takes the idea of your goal out of "wouldn't it be great" into "it will be wonderful when." In other words, it's what takes your goal from a dream into a reality.

When thinking about the story of success in your life, we talked about how you don't want to write the same chapter over and over again. Instead, you want to write a new chapter, a chapter filled with success after success after success.

In order for this to happen, you need to make the decision to do it. This isn't just a casual, "sure, I'll do it" type of decision. We're talking a real, things-are-gonna-be-different type of decision. This kind of decision sounds like:

I choose this for myself.

I choose to be abundant.

I choose to support my growth and expansion.

I choose to commit to my journey toward riches.

I decide that from this moment on my life will be different.

I decide to dedicate myself to my success.

I decide that from now on I will be more positive.

I decide that from now on I will take more positive actions and develop positive habits.

I decide to be wealthy.

I decide to be rich.

I decide to live my dreams.

Negative Motivation

One way to help keep you focused on what you want is to remind yourself from time to time what your life would be like if you don't make this big decision. What would happen? Would you go back to wishing and hoping for change? Would things stay the same? Would things actually get worse?

Remember those words from my mother: if you always do what you always did, you'll always get what you always got.

Are you ready for change?

Are you ready for more?

Are you really truly ready?

Are you ready to grow and change?

Are you ready to say, "Things will be different from now on!"?

Victim?
Or Victor?

Many people feel like they are a victim of their circumstances. They blame everyone around them, or the government, or other things for why they aren't experiencing the success they want. But you can always find someone who has a similar situation as yours and see how they have found great success. And you can also uncover people who have even more dramatic situations than what you have, and they have found great success.

You don't have to feel powerless. Whatever your circumstances are, there are positive thoughts and positive actions that can change them for the better. You are responsible for your own life, and you can absolutely make your life better and more successful.

If you read that last paragraph or two and thought, "Well that's easy for you to say, you aren't like me," then you are choosing to be a victim. How do I know? Because I used to do that. Instead, decide now that you are done being a victim of circumstances and you are ready to become a victor. No more victim consciousness. No more blaming others for your misery or lack or circumstances. Your boss is not responsible for your happiness or success. Your parents or family members are not responsible for your happiness or success. Your friends are not responsible for your happiness or success. Only *you* are responsible for your own happiness and success. (And, by the way, you aren't responsible for the happiness and success of other adults. Stay in your own lane!) If there is someone who you feel is causing you distress or limiting you in any way, then make a positive action to change it.

> Refuse to be held back, and you won't be held back.

Say: "I am not a victim of anyone or anything. I am the creator of my success!"

☞ DO THIS:
Take Three Actions

In an earlier section, I asked you to think of an action that you could take that would support your goal. Now I'm going to actually expand that a bit.

Without overthinking it, off the top of your head, what are three actions you could take right now that would have a positive effect on your life? Perhaps it's answering those emails, or cleaning out that closet, or calling that person, or paying those bills, or organizing your desk. These don't have to be big actions—just things that you could do that would make you feel great once they are done.

Often, these are things that we either do only after everything else is done or avoid altogether.

Write these things now below (or in your journal):

1._____

  _____

2._____

  _____

3._____

  _____

Your Inner Circle

Earlier, I asked you to write out your cast of characters. And then I asked you to note which ones were positive influences in your life, and which were negative. I did this for a reason. The people you surround yourself with have a huge influence on your life. These are the people we have allowed inside our circle, given our time and our presence to, and invited into our hearts.

There is a business idea that says that your success equals the average success of the five people you spend the most time with. If you hang out with people who talk a good game but mostly procrastinate, chances are you are the same. But if you surround yourself with people who are on the ball, who have confidence and love life, that vibe rubs off on you, and you will tend to have more confidence and success.

Your million-dollar mind needs support from the people in your life, as much as absolutely possible.

Now we are going to take this cast of characters one step further. This is a powerful exercise that can help you to reduce the amount of negativity you experience in your life. To clarify what I mean, negative people:

- **Drain you.**

- **Lower your energy.**

- **Don't see your potential.**

- **Complain.**

- **Are sarcastic.**

- **Talk about you behind your back.**

- **Aren't supportive.**

- **Are barriers to your success.**

If all the people in your life are positive and supportive, then good for you, you can go to the next section. But if you have negative people in your life, I have an exercise that can help.

A number of years ago, when I was trying to deal with the negative people in my life, I created a chart to help me see their influence. As a visual person, I needed something to look at that would help me to create more positivity and reduce the negativity I was experiencing. I call it a Relationship Circle.

In the chart on page 71, I want you to write the names of your cast of characters. The bullseye in the center is where you write the names of the people in your inner circle, those who are closest to you. The circle outside the inner circle contains the people who are next closest to you. And so on with each concentric circle, with the last circle being those people who are in your life but only on the edges. You aren't plotting the circles based on how close people are to you geographically, but rather emotionally. Who is currently in your inner circle? Who is in the outermost circle?

Now look at your Relationship Circle and notice which people bring positivity to your life and support you. In what circle are they located? And which people are negative and drain you of your energy? In what circle are those people?

I want you to do this exercise again, but this time write the names of those people who bring positivity in your life in your inner circle and write the names of the more negative people in one of the outer rings. And if there is someone who doesn't belong in any circle, then don't add them. Obviously, there are some people

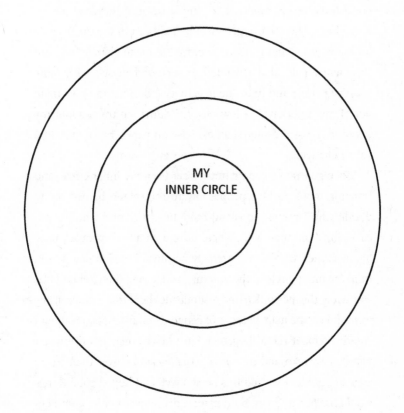

that we can't just cross off our list. But we can emotionally remove them from our inner circle.

When I first drew the circles for myself, I realized I had several people in my inner circle simply because they had always been there. These particular people had been in my inner circle for many years, and it hadn't occurred to me to change that. But then when I decided I wanted to surround myself with more positive people and limit the negativity, I decided to move them out of my inner circle a few rungs. I didn't tell them about my decision, I just did this as an exercise on paper, but it created a subtle change.

Moving negative people further out from my inner circle, and bringing more positive people toward the center, helped me to decide who I wanted to spend more time with and who I wanted to limit my time with. There were a couple of people in my life back then who were extremely negative. I moved one person from the inner circle to the outermost edge, and then I erased this and wrote this person's name just outside the furthest circle. They were still on the map, because of certain circumstances, meaning I couldn't remove them altogether. I just moved them to the furthest place on my map, and emotionally that meant I moved them to the edge of my life. I wished this person well and hoped good things would happen to them, but I made a decision to not let their negativity impact my life so deeply.

Again, I didn't tell this person I had done this exercise—frankly, to do so would have created drama and even more negativity, and that's what I was trying to minimize in my life. So instead I just spent less and less time with this person, and I stayed positive when I was with them. Another person I moved out of my inner circle was someone I cared for a lot, but I noticed that they were often absent when I needed them the most and when they were there, they were not always as supportive as I needed. I moved them to the circle just beyond the inner circle. And then I sat down with this person and expressed my feelings to them. I told them that I didn't feel as close to them, and why, and that I hoped that we could work through it. They didn't know I was feeling that way, and it was the opening we needed to get back on track. After our meeting, I moved this person back into the inner circle.

Create your second circle now.

How did it feel to redraw your circle based on who supports you and your journey best? How do you feel keeping the positive and supportive people in your inner circle, and the more negative people further out?

Review the following reminders to help you commit to your prosperous future and set yourself up for success:

Stop:

- Being wishy-washy.

- Avoiding making the decision to make more of your life.

- Letting negative people call the shots in your life.

- Being uncommitted in your own success.

- Being a victim.

Start:

- Being decisive.

- Spending more time with positive people who support you.

- Remembering that you are capable, brave, and strong.

- Believing you worthy of success.

☞ DO THIS:
Sign the Contract

If you are ready for your million-dollar future, then commit to it. I've made a little contract for you to sign, to make it official. (Well, not legally official, but it will feel more official to you.)

MY CONTRACT WITH MYSELF

I commit to my making my million-dollar future into my million-dollar reality.

I am 100% responsible for my own life.

I commit now to positive thoughts and actions that support my growth in all areas of my life, including my finances.

I am ready. It is time.

I commit myself now.

X _____

Date _____

Part
Two

Act Like a Millionaire

There is nothing
worse than
unrealized potential.

Begin Now, Not Later

Congratulations! You've completed the first half of your success story. You are well on your way to creating a millionaire mind, the mindset for riches. In Part One of the book we did the mental groundwork, now we start taking action. And we begin with the principle of taking action *now*, not later.

It's common to talk about your hopes and dreams as if they'll happen in some amorphous future. You might say things like:

Someday I'd like to . . .

Maybe at one point I can . . .

When I'm older, I will . . .

In this chapter, we move our success from some time in the future to creating our success now, day by day, action by action.

Energy Follows Action

It would be great if we took action once we felt motivated to do so. But that's just not the way life works. The formula is actually the reverse. **We'll feel the motivation once we take action.**

Here's a simple analogy. If you only went to the gym when you felt motivated to do so, then what kind of results would you see? Probably not very dramatic results. But anyone who has committed to going to the gym consistently will tell you that there are some (many? most?) days when they didn't want to go to the gym, but once they did go to the gym, they felt so good afterward and that in turn motivated them to keep going and to go even more. The energy/feeling/motivation came after going to the gym. **The energy/feeling/motivation for your success will come after you take actions toward it.**

Don't believe me? Give it try.

Everything Begins
with Action

Before you take action, everything is a theory. After you take action, you are in the process of moving toward something. **There is nothing worse than unrealized potential.** Wouldn't it be terrible to come to the end of your life and think, "I wish I had wasted less time procrastinating and taken more actions and chances . . ."? It doesn't have to be that way.

You've already decided to commit to your million-dollar journey, and today is the day you are going to take it from theory to process. Again, using that analogy of the gym, you can think about joining and going to a gym for weeks and months, but thinking about it won't actually change anything. Once you go, even after your first workout, your body begins changing. And after you went that first time, it was easier to go the second day, and the third. That's because you created momentum with that first action.

☞ DO THIS:
Take Action Now

Good news, you already know which actions to take! You might be thinking: I do?! Yes, you do!

If you remember, one of the exercises in a previous chapter was to write three actions you could take immediately that would have a positive effect on your life. What I'm going to ask you to do now is to go do those three things. If you can do them at this very moment, close this book and do them. Or do them as soon as you can.

Now, go do what you can right now. Go on . . . I'll wait here for you.

Welcome back. How did it feel to take those actions?

While those three actions may or may not have had a direct connection to your goal, they do constitute actions, and taking actions changes both how you feel and your circumstances.

☞ DO THIS: Take Three (More Actions)

Now that you took three actions, I want you to stay with that energy of action. So below, write down three more actions you can take tomorrow. Remember, these are off the top of your head; don't overthink it. Write them down now:

1._____

_____

2._____

_____

3._____

_____

If you want, you can do some of those actions today. However, I want you to get in the habit of doing today's actions today and letting tomorrow's actions happen tomorrow. Why? First, because I don't want you to become overwhelmed. It's always true that when we start something new we have a lot of energy and want to do as much as possible. But if we do more and more up front, I've noticed that people then tend to be overwhelmed very quickly, and give up on their journey. Their commitment wanes, and even stops. Second, getting in the habit of just doing today's actions today allows us to create healthy habits right from the start. It's called "balance." **The more balance you create right now, from the start, the more success you will have.** Why? Because you are starting from a position of strength and wholeness, which will continue to fuel you further.

Also, get in the habit of creating actions to take and writing them down. Like everything else in this book, the simpler you make it, the better. One of my students was so excited after the first class on Prosperity Principles that on the way home he stopped at an office supply store and bought a very complicated planner—one that had many tabs, special paper that only fit that planner, an expensive leather cover, a special pen that fit in a penholder in that planner, and so on. He showed everyone at the next class this whole setup, and when I asked him how much he spent on it, he said it was well over a hundred dollars. You can already guess the end of this story. By the end of the class, he wasn't using the planner. He said it was . . . wait for it . . . too complicated. Remember KISSS? Keep it simple, super simple!

Now, if you love complicated planners, by all means use one. Go for it. Some people do love that level of structure. However, if you're one of those people who think you need to make things complicated—including your actions toward success—**complicating things sabotages your success.**

How I Keep Track of Actions

Whatever system you use to track actions, just do it. What do I do? There are two things that work for me. First, I carry a journal around with me all the time, and I write down things that come to mind, including actions that I need to take. Second, I use sticky notes. Everything I need to do, I write it on a sticky note. One action per note. And when I do that action, I crumple up that sticky note and throw it away. It's very satisfying to do! (By the way, you can take notes on your phone and on your computer if you don't want to use paper sticky notes).

If an action that I need to take is too big for one sticky note, I see what smaller actions I need to take first, write the sticky notes for those, and then keep doing that until the larger action is done. Remember, big how, little how? Breaking bigger actions into smaller, achievable ones supports your million-dollar journey.

I'm not telling you to do it like I do. I'm telling you how I do it to inspire you to find the way that works for you. I've used this system to write many books, do all I do for my very complicated and detail-oriented job, for my family, for everything. It works.

Daily Actions,
Daily Check-in

Do your actions each day. At night, reflect on the day and review your action items. Here are some of the questions you can ask yourself:

- **Did you do them all?**

- **If not, what did you not do?**

- **And why?**

- **Were you avoiding it?**

- **Were you overwhelmed?**

- **Would it have helped to break the action you didn't take into smaller actions that were more achievable?**

- **Is your system of keeping track of actions working for you?**

- **What do you need to change?**

- **What do you need help with?**

- **Who can you ask for that help?**

- **Do you feel good about the actions you took?**

- **Did you do too much?**

- **Did you not do enough?**

- **What could you do better tomorrow?**

Checking in keeps you accountable and also keeps your goals at the forefront of your mind. Remember, what you give your attention to is what is more apt to happen.

Yin or Yang

When it comes to actions, some people are more yin and some are more yang. You might have seen a yin-yang symbol, it looks like this:

Yang, the white side of the symbol, is described as the "masculine" aspect of the yin-yang symbol. It's the more action-oriented, active, giving part of the symbol. Yin, the black side of the symbol, is described as the "feminine" aspect of the yin-yang symbol. It's the more inward, passive, nurturing part of the symbol.

Both parts together create one whole. The whole needs both parts in order to be complete. This is the symbol for our lives. We need both yin and yang aspects in our lives to be whole, to be in balance.

Some people are out of balance. Some people tend to be more yin, and some tend to be more yang. Here are qualities of both:

YIN	YANG
Passive	Active
Feminine energy	Masculine energy
Inward	Outward
Be-er	Doer
Relaxed	Intense
Easygoing	Demanding
Gentle	Assertive
Spontaneous	Planned
Subtle	Direct
Flexible	Decisive
Procrastinator	Busy-Making

Do you identify with aspects of both? Or do you identify more with one or the other. I personally tend to be more yang oriented in life. I'm a doer, a planner, more outwardly focused. I've found that I sometimes need to do less in order to be more balanced, which paradoxically allows me to do more.

On the other hand, I've seen people who are more yin oriented. They are more relaxed, subtle, and can be procrastinators. They sometimes need to do more in order to be more balanced, which allows them to experience more success.

Why is this important? Especially here, in the chapter about action?

If you are more yang, then you need to:

- Watch so you are not overdoing each day.

- Not procrastinate in the form of "keeping busy" (but not doing what you really need to do).

- Not overwhelm yourself.

- Take time each day to relax, meditate, do something calming.

- Connect with yourself and with other people.

- Let others help you at times.

- Be rigid or overthinking.

- Remember that you need to "be" and not just "do."

If you are more yin, then you need to:

- **Choose to take actions toward your goal every day.**

- **Watch so you are not avoiding or procrastinating actions.**

- **Connect with your goal, and be creative each day to move toward it.**

- **Assert yourself at times.**

- **Be direct about your wants and needs.**

- **Watch so you won't be depressed or needy.**

- **Not withdraw.**

- **Not let fear stop you.**

- **Not feel like a victim.**

- **Remember that you need to "do" and not just "be."**

Do you feel balanced? Or do you feel more of a yin? Or more of a yang? Write your answer here or in your journal:

_____

_____

_____

_____

_____

_____

The Key to the Most Effective Action

Here's a secret about taking action. When you approach your list of actions for the day, do the hardest one first. **Do the thing that you least want to do first.** Why? It's the opposite of what most people do. Most people tend to look at their action list and do the easy things first, and then by the time they do those things, they either don't have time or energy (or both) to do the bigger, harder things. **If you start with the hardest thing first, you create incredible momentum for the rest of your day, and you will be likelier to get everything done.** Don't believe me? Try it and see!

The Power of Auto-Suggestion

Some of the first books on prosperity and success mention the word "auto-suggestion" as a key to master to achieve what you want. What is auto-suggestion? Very simply put, auto-suggestion is repeating something over and over again to create a certain outcome. When you consciously feed suggestions to your subconscious mind, it gets to work on orienting your life toward what you are feeding it.

> # We are what we think about all day long.

Everyone uses auto-suggestion already. One prosperity teacher explained it this way: **we are what we think about all day long.** If we don't learn how to train our way of thinking and our thoughts, then we tend to do what I call "faux think"—which is to just think about whatever is in front of us and not what's ahead of us or the bigger picture. **Auto-suggestion is a way to influence our outcomes and actions by flooding our mind with specific thoughts.**

One study I read a few years ago said that we are surrounded by seven times more negative imagery and information in the media than positive imagery and information. Seven times! If that's true, then that means that to balance out the negativity, we need to flood our mind with positivity as much as we can.

If we think negative thoughts most of the day, then we are using auto-suggestion in a negative way. That's negative auto-suggestion. **The good news is that we can consciously choose what we feed our mind. We can choose to saturate our mind with positive auto-suggestion, positive self-talk.** It's as simple as coming up with ways to put as many positive ideas into our mind as possible. The more positivity you put into your mind, the more positivity that comes out. That's common sense, but that doesn't mean it's easy. If it were easy to have a positive outlook, we'd all be positive all the time! And we wouldn't use negativity to create drama and attention, and then wonder why we have a negative experience.

Auto-suggestion is vitally important to your goal. You need to make sure to create self-talk that is congruent with your goal. In other words, you need think in ways that support your goal. How do you use auto-suggestion to do this? You find ways to repeat messages that reflect a positive outcome.

For example, if your goal is to make one million dollars by the end of the year, because it will allow you to be completely out of debt and make you feel prosperous, then you create a series of statements that reflect that, such as:

- **I am a millionaire.**

- **I deserve to prosper and succeed.**

- **I am a magnet for the good that I desire.**

- **I already feel like a millionaire and express this in all I do.**

- **I take positive actions every day and experience positive results.**

- **I choose to see situations and experiences in a positive way.**

- **Positivity is my path; prosperity is my result.**

And so on. You can create as many of these auto-suggestions as you want. Then find as many ways as you can to feed these thoughts to your mind.

You can:

- **Write them in your journal every day—maybe choose a few of them and write them over and over again in your journal each day.**

- **Write them on sticky notes (one per note) and place those notes around your home and office/workplace (if possible).**

- **Make a recording of yourself speaking these statements and listen to it over and over (all smartphones have this function).**

- **Download positive success affirmations (you can purchase these online from iTunes, Amazon, or even from your local bookstore).**

What other ways can you feed these positive thoughts into your mind? Write these ways down here (or in your journal):

_____

_____

_____

_____

_____

_____

☞ DO THIS: Write Your Auto-Suggestions

Now that you know about auto-suggestion, it's time for you to create your own statements, to feed your mind and support your journey to success. In the space below, or in your journal, write at least five statements that support your goal.

1. _____
2. _____
3. _____
4. _____
5. _____

And now write down three ways you can use these statements to immerse them into your subconscious mind (i.e., memorize them, write them on sticky notes, etc.)

1. _____
2. _____
3. _____

The Law of Giving and Receiving

You may have heard about the Law of Attraction, the Law of Karma, or the Law of Cause and Effect. These three laws of life all say the same thing. Simply put, these laws essentially teach that what you give is what you receive. If you put forth negativity, you'll receive negativity. If you put forth positivity, you'll receive positivity. The Bible says it this way: as you sow, so shall you reap. Spiritual teachers will often say that every action creates energy. When we choose actions that create joy and positivity, we see the fruit of our actions as more joy and positivity in our lives. A version of this law can be found in most of the world's wisdom traditions and from some philosophers. These are not mathematical laws, but rather mental laws to help us create more of what we want. When we are aligned in our thoughts and actions toward a goal, that goal is likelier to happen. It's common sense to realize that our actions cause reactions. Therefore . . .

Whatever it is you want more of, start giving it first.

Another name for this law is the Law of Giving and Receiving. **You'll notice that this is not the Law of Receiving and then Giving.**

The Giving comes first. I discussed this earlier in the section about the formula for life, which is: **energy follows action.** This is another way to think about that formula and use it on your journey.

How can you use the Law of Giving and Receiving in your own life? I'll tell you how I used it in mine. When I first heard about this law, I wanted to test it, so I started with love. When I wanted more love, I gave love first and was easily able to see more love flowing back to me. What I really wanted at one point in my life was more money, but I just couldn't bring myself to think about giving. After all, I had so little, and had such a huge debt. Giving seemed to be the opposite of what I needed to do. I rationalized that I would give once I had something to give.

A speaker I once heard at a conference summed it up best. She said that **the Law of Giving and Receiving worked in the way we worked it. If we used the law sporadically, we would see sporadic results. If we used this life law consistently and joyfully, then we would see consistent and joyful results.** That's true of anything in life, isn't it? Remember the analogy of the gym? If you go sporadically, you will see limited results. But if you go to the gym consistently and with enthusiasm, you'll see more results, and you'll see them more quickly.

I decided that I wanted to be a generous person. I began by making a small donation to my church consistently, every week. Granted, it wasn't very much, some weeks it was just a dollar or two, though at that time in my life, a dollar or two meant a great deal. It brought me great joy to be able to give, to be generous. Consequently, life started being generous with me. A friend would pick up the check at lunch, or I would get a small raise, or I would find a little money in a pocket of my trousers. While I couldn't prove that these things happened directly as a result of my giving, my intuition told me that I was placing myself in a generous stream of life. By giving, I started to take notice when I was receiving. It's certainly possible that those things would have happened anyway, but I think **by developing the muscle of giving, I was also developing the muscle to notice the many ways that I received from the world.**

The more I gave, the more I received. Eventually I committed myself to consistent giving, sharing a portion of all the income I received with places, people, and organizations that inspired me. It became (and has become) a joyous practice to give to others. **I always give to a person or place that has inspired me to become greater than I was before or has somehow inspired me.** I don't give out of obligation, that wouldn't be in keeping with the spirit that the law intends. I think of it as giving from my bounty.

☞ DO THIS: Practice the Law of Giving and Receiving

Answer the following questions in your journal:

> What do you want more of? Your answer is what you need to begin giving.

> How do you want to give? Each week? Each month? Each time you are paid?

> What people or organizations inspire you?

Decide a reasonable amount to give to one of the people or organizations on your list. Start small, you can increase later.

Give. Start today. Enact the Law of Giving and Receiving. Do it right now. I often like to write a note to the person or organization to include with a check or cash, but you can also give online. Decide what makes you happiest to give and do that.

Giving is a voluntary activity that can create a lot of joy. **Every self-made millionaire I know has made a great habit of giving, and it certainly seems as if they receive much in return.**

Review the following powerful reminders to help you take consistent, positive action.

Stop:

- Finding ways to numb yourself or procrastinate.

- Delaying your actions until "tomorrow" or "later."

- Waiting until you feel motivated or inspired before taking action.

- Filling your life with negative thoughts and negative people.

Start:

- Making positive actions a habit.

- Making a list of today's actions, and doing the hardest one first.

- Using the practice of auto-suggestion to flood your life with positivity.

- Using the Law of Giving and Receiving.

Every
self-made millionaire
I know has made
a great habit of giving,
and it certainly seems
as if they receive much
in return.

Many of us are enthusiastic beginners. It's harder to stay motivated.

Take Steps Every Single Day

Are you great at starting new projects?

Are you the type of person who sticks with something until you finish it?

Do you sometimes start things and lose interest sometime thereafter?

Do you tend to talk about what you do more than you do it?

Do you have several unfinished projects?

Do you begin something new and then stop when it gets complicated or you don't know what to do next?

Do you think that you need to do all the work, because you want it "done right"?

If you said "yes" to any of the above, you aren't alone. In fact, you're in the majority. Many of us are enthusiastic beginners. It's harder to stay motivated, to stay the course until we reach our goals.

Every self-made millionaire will tell you that their journey had twists and turns, ebbs and flows, and highs and lows. The beginning of the journey is fresh and new and can be fun. Your energy is high, and off you go. And then, tedium sets in. Or you hit a bump in the road. Or you get distracted by other things. Or you procrastinate. Or . . . it could be a million other things.

Whether your goal is financial, entrepreneurial, creative, or anything at all, everything begins as a dream. However, **a dream is a dream until you begin it, and then it becomes a responsibility.** Once it's a responsibility, it's your responsibility! This is a truth that I came to realize.

It's natural to want the journey to riches to be easy and painless. Unfortunately, that's not realistic. However, if you expect that your journey will include highs and lows, then you won't be surprised and you can prepare yourself, which will minimize the chances that you will give up before you reach your goal.

Flow and Ebb

Have you read or heard about the state of "flow"? It's a psycholog-
ical idea described as being so immersed in an activity, that time
seems to stop. You are completely focused on what you are doing.
Sometimes it is called being "in the zone," fully absorbed in what
you are doing.

When have you experienced that state of flow? What activities
do you do that put you in that state? For some people it's garden-
ing, or reading, or taking walks in nature, or painting, or meditat-
ing. For each person, it's different. Write down some activities that
put you in a state of flow.

Self-made millionaires often talk about being in a state of flow
while they are working toward their goal. After all, they usually
create their wealth by doing something they love to do.

Being in a state of flow is wonderful. Choosing to do those activities that put you in that state is a good idea. But, **being in a state
of flow is only half of the story.** As much as we all would love to
be in the state of flow all the time, it just doesn't happen that way.
Flow is one half of the whole. The other half of the equation is ebb.

When people use the word "ebb," it's usually to denote a negative state of being. They might describe their energy as ebbing or
they might say, "Our company sales have ebbed." It's used as the
opposite of flow, and people wish they didn't experience it.

I don't see ebb in that way. I see ebb as the partner of flow. **Ebb and flow: two halves of a whole.** If there is a positive association attached to flow, then let's attach a positive association to ebb as well. After all, it's a state of being we *will* find ourselves in from time to time.

The ocean doesn't just flow. It ebbs. That doesn't mean something is wrong with it. It only means that in one part of the world, the ocean is ebbing at that moment (and in another part of the world, that same ocean is flowing). Some coasts and beaches of the world are in flood tide while other coasts and beaches are in ebb tide. It's a cycle—and it's natural.

Similarly, different parts of our life can be in a state of flow, while others can be in ebb. It's normal and natural.

What you do during an ebb time, however, can move you closer to your goal. During an ebb state you might tend to procrastinate, avoid your daily commitments, or give in to sluggish inactivity. However, now that you know an ebb state is normal, you can choose to experience it differently. Think of flow as summer and ebb as winter. You can be productive and effective in both seasons, even though they are very different (at least where I live!).

Ebb is a time to do four main things: renew, review, revise, and recommit. In a nutshell, in ebb we have less energy and focus (it's the opposite of flow), so that's why it's a good time to:

- **Renew**—find ways to nurture yourself and refill your energy tanks.

- **Review**—look at your plans and actions to see if you are still on course.

- **Revise**—make any changes and adjustments to your plans and your actions.

- **Recommit**—consciously dedicate yourself once again to being focused on your goal.

Be Consistent

Self-made millionaires develop certain million-dollar habits. One of them is the habit of being consistent. If you ask any self-made millionaire, they will tell you that they made their goal a priority and worked on it consistently, usually every day.

If you have a big goal, but you only want to work on it when you "feel like it" or for just an hour a week, chances are you aren't going to reach your goal anytime soon. If that's the level of commitment you want to give it, perhaps you haven't chosen a big enough or juicy enough goal to work toward.

You should want what you want so much that you are willing to commit time every day to accomplish it. Yes, take time off to rest so you stay balanced. Just make sure that you develop the habit of taking actions toward your goal consistently.

The more consistent you are, the faster you will reach your goal. I've known self-made millionaires who worked on their goal while they also had a full-time job and other responsibilities. How? They woke up an hour early to devote time to working toward their goal. Or they stayed up an hour late (if they aren't morning people!). Or they worked during their lunchtime, or between classes, or when the kids were asleep or in school, or some other time they carved out of their lives.

Be Persistent

The sibling of "consistent" is "persistent." **Consistent means doing something every day. Persistent means doing those things when you don't want to.**

Yes, you are going to have days where you don't want to work toward your goal. Let's go back to the gym analogy. When you begin to work out in a gym, it's new and exciting and you are filled with the dream of building a healthier, stronger body. The first few days are new, you're in learning mode. After a few weeks the novelty of starting something new wears off. Plus, you are sore, so sore! You wake up one morning, intending to go to the gym, but your bed is so warm, and you feel so sore, and . . . it's snowing outside. Going to the gym is going to take a herculean effort on your part. The temptation to stay home just that one day is strong. "Just for today," you think, "I'll go back again tomorrow." Decision made, you go back to sleep all warm and snug. Throughout that day, you notice that you are sore, but you don't have that endorphin rush you get after going to the gym. Oh well, you think, I'll go back tomorrow.

Then tomorrow morning comes and you think, "Well, I loved sleeping in yesterday, maybe I'll just let myself do it again and anyway, it's snowing again." Restarting the action of going to the gym gets harder each day that you don't do it.

There will be days like this on your journey toward your goal. There will be times when you want to take a breather. There will be times when it snows (literally or figuratively)! **Those are the days that you need to double down and take those actions toward your goal.** Those who end up getting out of bed and going to the gym despite their feelings and the snow will say that it was the best thing they did, and afterward they were glad they pushed through the inertia and stayed on course. Their goal of health and fitness is one step closer *because* of their persistence.

> You will be one step closer to your goal if you develop the million-dollar habit of persistence.

Successful People
Are Consistent and Persistent

Many years ago, I attended a writers' workshop. The daylong conference featured a variety of authors, editors, and other publishing professionals talking to novice and wannabe writers about how best to hone their skills and potential to get published.

During one of the lectures, an editor was talking about special skills that writers develop. At one point she said something about Danielle Steel, the famous romance writer who, as I write this book, has written over 180 books! Danielle Steel isn't a writer who is often reviewed in the *New York Times* and isn't considered to be a "literary" writer.

Romance writers don't always get as much respect as they deserve. So when this editor happened to mention Danielle Steel in passing, there was a reaction in the audience. Some of the audience members laughed a little, some rolled their eyes, and some murmured something to the person next to them. The editor who was speaking noticed, and she immediately stopped her lecture. "What?" she asked, "what did I say?" There was silence, and then someone yelled out, "You mentioned Danielle Steel, she's not a real writer!" There was some laughter of agreement in the audience. The editor said, "And you all are real writers?" Some audience members yelled out "yes."

The editor put down her lecture notes and looked right at the audience. Then she said something I've never forgotten, even now, over thirty years later. She said, "Do you want to know the difference between you and Danielle Steel?" There were some smirking faces and a little more laughter from the audience. And then the editor said, **"Danielle Steel writes every day, and you don't."**

There was dead silence as her sentence landed. It was like a knockout punch. Here were all these unpublished "writers" who were hoping to get published someday, and they were putting down a writer who was so dedicated to her craft, whether others applauded her or not, that she had at that point written dozens of books, nearly all of which had hit the bestseller lists. Danielle Steel wasn't (and isn't) a success by accident. To this day, she is consistent in her writing habits. And if you read a story about her, you will find that she continued to write her novels even during the most difficult times of her life (five marriages and divorces, nine children, the death of a child, and various other ups and downs). Through it all, she was consistent and persistent. She is now the fourth best-selling fiction author of all time, and her novels have sold nearly a billion copies. And, for the record, she's a real writer.

Be inspired by every successful person. Let their success inspire you to be more dedicated, more consistent, and more persistent when times get tough.

Recognize Chemicalization

What happens when, as you move toward your goal, things start going wrong? What happens when it seems like, despite all of your consistent and persistent efforts, the opposite of what you want starts showing up in your life? Perhaps unexpected bills pop up. Or you discover an accounting error. Or an unplanned hurdle suddenly makes itself known. It could be any number of things that look like the opposite of what you want.

Those things might make you think you are on the wrong path, or that you have chosen the wrong goal. They might also make you think that you are doing something wrong, or that success goes to others and not to you.

I've got good news for you. It might just be something called **chemicalization.**

I first encountered the principle of chemicalization while studying the teachings of early New Thought teacher Emma Curtis Hopkins. Over a hundred years ago, she wrote in her book *Scientific Christian Mental Practice*, "When a physical or mental disturbance arises, as the effect of opposing Truth, it is called chemicalization. It is always met by keeping right on with the Truth. It is always the sign that Truth is working fast." She goes on to write, "You may be interested to know that chemicalization means that things are coming out in a better state of affairs. It never means anything else. It is like alkali and acid in chemistry. When they mix they form a new base. There is nothing to fear, there is no pain in chemicalization. There is no sorrow, if you do not believe in such things."

Let me rephrase that in today's terms, and with our focus here:

As you work toward your goal, if anything arises that looks contrary to what you want, it is chemicalization at work. This can be a sign that you are on the right track. Chemicalization means that things are working to rearrange themselves in your favor. If you look at what's happening through the lens of chemicalization, then you can relax and know you are headed in the right direction. Rather than stop you, let the chemicalization inspire you with the knowledge that it's all working.

When these "disturbances" show up in your life, here's what I suggest:

- **Don't panic.**

- **Reframe it as something that is working in your favor, even if you can't see how (yet).**

- **Take swift, positive action toward your goal.**

Don't let anything stop you! Reframe everything as something that is bringing your goal to you even faster. Remember: **self-made millionaires develop the skill of turning negatives into positives.**

How You Start Your Day Matters

Do you wake up in the morning, and think, "Oh god, another day, I wish I could just stay in bed." And then you watch the morning news while you make your coffee, read the newspaper, spend some time on social media, bemoan all the bad news, and then wonder why you aren't feeling more upbeat and positive?

This is how millions of people begin their day. But it's the exact opposite of how most self-made millionaires begin their day.

What would happen if you woke up, and first thing, you read your goal that you had written out and kept by your bedside? Next, you ate a healthy breakfast while you reviewed the actions that you need to make for the day. Following that, you decided which action was the most difficult, or the one that you dread doing the most, and then did that action first. If you began your day in this way, how do you think the rest of your day would go? Chances are you would be rested, focused, inspired, and after doing that most difficult thing first, you will have created incredible momentum for the rest of the day.

In the space below, or in your journal, write what you do first thing in the morning:

_____

_____

_____

_____

_____

_____

Now write down how you would like to change your morning routine so that it focuses you and better supports you as you work toward your goal:

_____

_____

_____

_____

_____

_____

Tomorrow morning start your new routine. If you have to wake up a little earlier to do so, then remember to set your clock.

How You End
Your Day Matters

It's also important how you end your day. While starting your day off positively and focused on your goal will create great momentum during the day, how you end your day can help you toward your goal as well.

One self-made millionaire described her bedtime routine to me, and it inspired me to change mine. Here's her routine:

- **Begin winding down at around 8 p.m.**

- **Go to the bedroom around 10 p.m., and reflect on the day.**

- **Note the things I did well.**

- **Note what I didn't do, avoided, or that didn't turn out the way I wanted.**

- **Think of some actions to take the following morning.**

- **Read my written goal that I keep by my bedside.**

- **Fall asleep thinking of the positive statements that supported me in reaching my goal.**

That made such an impression on me, and sounded so positive, that I decided to emulate her. I do roughly the same procedure most nights, and it's made a huge difference in my life. Falling asleep in such a positive way infuses my subconscious with focus and positivity. It also helps to create an atmosphere of positivity when I wake up.

In the space below, or in your journal, describe your bedtime routine.

_____

_____

_____

_____

_____

_____

How can you alter your bedtime routine to support you in positive ways?

_____

_____

_____

_____

_____

_____

Start this new routine tonight.

What You Do Between Waking Up and Going to Bed Matters

Of course, the most important time of your day, in terms of reaching your goal, is throughout your daily activities. How do you plan on moving toward your goal over the course of the day? Here are some ideas for structuring your day to do that:

- Do your new morning routine, as you wrote above.

- Remember to write your actions, and then do the hardest one first, which will create momentum.

- Continue to do the actions you wrote on your list for that day.

- Make sure to have healthy snacks around, and take time for lunch.

- Every so often take a break, take a quick walk around the block, or spend some time in nature.

- If possible, don't stay signed-in to your email all day—email will distract you from other activities. Take 15-minute email breaks, where you sign into your email, answer messages, and then sign off.

- Save internet browsing and social media as a reward for completing the day's tasks.

- If you have a meeting, stay on topic and keep it as concise as possible.

- Keep your positive statements (auto-suggestions) on sticky notes throughout your home and work space.

What other ways can you think of to support yourself during the day as you work toward your goal?

_____

_____

_____

_____

_____

_____

☞ DO THIS:
Get Unstuck

Sometimes we can do all the right things, and yet we still occasionally feel stuck. It's at these times that we feel that we have hit a wall, and either don't have the motivation to move forward, or feel like we don't know how to move forward (or both). Here is a surefire way to break through this stuck feeling.

- **Step One: get your journal or a sheet of paper and a pen.**

- **Step Two: sit somewhere comfortable, where you won't be disturbed.**

- **Step Three: make a list of all the things that are unfinished in your life (see below for some ideas).**

- **Step Four: write a #1 next to the thing you least want to do, a #2 next to the next least thing you want to do, and so on.**

- **Step Five: go do the thing that you wrote #1 next to.**

Do all of this as quickly as you can. Don't overthink it.

The unfinished items for Step Three don't have to relate specifically to your goal. They could be anything unfinished in your life. Some of the things that I have written down include: laundry, clean out the closet, pay bills, schedule healthcare appointments (dentist, yearly physical, etc.), take out the garbage, reply to that email, call a relative, mail a birthday card, etc., etc., etc.!

When you are stuck, the act of finishing something remotivates you and creates new momentum so that you can go back to your goal with eagerness and energy.

How does this exercise relate to your goal? Good question. Here are some ways that it helps you on your journey to riches:

- **Feeling stuck is sometimes a way we procrastinate, and that is a form of self-sabotage.**

- **Finishing something is a form of positive self-care.**

- **Taking positive action on anything creates positive energy and forward momentum that you can then use in a focused way.**

Finishing even one thing on your list will likely get you unstuck and back on track.

Daily Gratitude

You may have heard about keeping a daily list of things you are grateful for. From books featured on Oprah to top business books to articles in magazines of all kinds, keeping a "gratitude list" has become a common practice.

I remember giving a prosperity workshop a few years back, and one of the participants raised his hand. He explained that he was feeling blocked and unmotivated in life and wondered if there was something he could do that would help. I suggested that he keep a daily gratitude list for the next week and see how that brought positivity to his life. He looked at me condescendingly, and then said, "Yes, I know all about gratitude lists. I kept one of those years ago when they first became the trend."

I was amused that he thought that keeping a gratitude list was so passé. I asked him, "Well, if you know about them, and have kept one, do you keep a list now?" "No," replied, "been there, done that." My answer? "And yet here you are, feeling blocked and unmotivated. Maybe it's time to try a gratitude list again?" The lightbulb went off in his head, and he sat down, a little sheepishly.

The next week, this same guy came to class, raised his hand at the beginning of class, and told us that he had thought about what I had said in class. He went home right away and began keeping a daily gratitude list, one that he really spent time on and was thoughtful about (as opposed to just writing down five things as fast as he could). He then told us that it really did have a positive effect on his mood during the week, and that the first thing he put on that day's gratitude list was . . . making a gratitude list!

Like anything, a gratitude list is as powerful as you make it. If you take time each day to focus on what's positive, on what's working right, on what brings you joy, this focus will in turn create a greater sense of meaning and happiness in your life.

The feeling of gratitude:

- **Magnetizes you to experience more.**

- **Makes you happier and more productive.**

- **Creates greater meaning for everything and everyone in your life.**

- **Allows you to see even things you used to think as negative with a new lens.**

- **Will help to create even more things and people you feel grateful for in the future.**

☞ DO THIS:
Keep a Gratitude List

In your journal, write something like "I'm Grateful for . . ." at the top of a clean page.

Next, take a breath to focus and center yourself.

And then begin to write down everything that comes to mind that you are grateful for.

Don't judge anything you write as too silly, too small, too odd; just put down what comes to mind.

It doesn't matter how many things you write down—whether you list one thing or thirty things doesn't matter; what matters is that you truly feel deep gratitude for what you include.

When your list feels complete, take a moment to read through it, and silently (or aloud) say thank you to each person and experience that you wrote down.

Repeat daily.

Do this for just one week and see what happens! Gratitude lifts your mood and makes you feel more fulfilled. In turn, this helps you move toward your goal. I don't know one self-made millionaire that doesn't take time to feel grateful.

☞ DO THIS: Reward Yourself Along the Way

Many self-made millionaires find ways to stay motivated, including rewarding their efforts along the way, or creating a reward for when they reach a goal. Here's the thing: anything positive that keeps you on track toward reaching your goal is something you should do. Some of the rewards that I or people I've known have used as an incentive to reach a goal include:

A trip to someplace wonderful (Europe? Vegas? Tropical resort? Safari?)

A bottle of their favorite wine (or Irish whiskey ☺)

Dinner at a favorite restaurant

A concert

A special pen from Montblanc (or another pen company)

A new car

A weekend at a spa

A quiet weekend at home (to sleep late!)

A party

What reward would you choose when you reach your goal? Write it below:

_____

_____

What steps can you take now to prepare? For example, if you chose a vacation in Rome, maybe take a few minutes to do research which hotel or Airbnb you would stay in and bookmark that page for future use. Print out photos of the hotel and landmarks you want to visit in the city, and post these where you can see them often. The more you see them, the more they will motivate you.

Your Creative Mind

Need some inspiration? Need some ideas for actions that you can take to bring you closer to your goal? Wondering about what next steps to take?

I happened upon a great way to mine the depths of my mind for ideas while reading Napoleon Hill's *Think and Grow Rich*. In the book Hill tells the story of "the late Dr. Elmer R. Gates, of Chevy Chase, Maryland." Here is what he wrote:

> [Dr. Gates] created more than two hundred useful patents, many of them basic, through the process of cultivating and using the creative faculty. His method is both significant and interesting to one interested in attaining to the status of genius, in which category Dr. Gates unquestionable belonged. Dr. Gates was one of the really great, though less publicized scientists of the world.
>
> In his laboratory, he had what he called his "personal communication room." It was practically sound proof, and so arranged that all light could be shut out. It was equipped with a small table, on which he kept a pad of writing paper. In front of the table, on the wall, was an electric pushbutton, which controlled the lights. When Dr. Gates desired to draw upon the forces available to him through his creative imagination, he would go into this room, seat himself

at the table, shut off the lights, and concentrate upon the known factors of the invention on which he was working, remaining in that position until ideas began to "flash" into his mind in connection with the unknown factors of the invention.

On one occasion, ideas came through so fast that he was forced to write for almost three hours. When the thoughts stopped flowing, and he examined his notes, he found they contained a minute description of principles which had not a parallel among the known data of the scientific world. Moreover, the answer to his problem was intelligently presented in those notes. In this manner Dr. Gates completed over two hundred patents...

Dr. Gates earned his living by "sitting for ideas'" for individuals and corporations. Some of the largest corporations in America paid him substantial fees, by the hour, for "sitting for ideas."

The reasoning faculty is often faulty, because it is largely guided by one's accumulated experience. Not all knowledge, which one accumulates through "experience," is accurate. Ideas received through the creative faculty are much more reliable, for the reason that they come from sources more reliable than any which are available to the reasoning faculty of the mind.

There is plenty of reliable evidence that the faculty of creative imagination exists.

What does all this mean? Here's a brief distillation:

- **Dr. Gates sat in a dark room with a pad of paper and pencil.**

- **He would think of a problem.**

- **He would sit there until he thought of a solution, and then wrote down anything and everything that came to mind.**

- **He earned a lot of money by tapping into his creative imagination.**

I must have reread that story ten times before I thought to myself, "Wait a second, I can do this, too!"

☞ DO THIS:
Sit for Ideas

Sit down in a comfortable spot with your journal and a pen.

Take a few breaths to focus and calm yourself.

Think of a variation on the question "What is mine to do today, toward the goal?"

Keep breathing.

As ideas of action items come to mind, write them down (even if they seem unrelated to my goal).

When you feel the list is complete, look it over and begin doing all the items you wrote down.

This has been one of the most creative ways I have found to decide what actions I need to take toward my goal. It's also a wonderful way of tapping into my inner wisdom. Some people might feel the inspiration comes from somewhere else (God, the Universe, etc.), but I feel it's a way of bypassing my rational mind and getting to my creative mind. Sometimes our rational, conscious mind is fixed on what it can see, but the creative part of our brain can think "outside the box" and come up with ideas that are different than what our rational mind might come up with.

This is an extremely easy activity that can yield surprisingly huge results. Give it a try for a few days and see how it can help you, too.

Stop:

- Giving up when things get difficult.

- Feeling like you have no options or don't know what to do.

- Feeling ungrateful for your life and all in it.

Start:

- Finishing things that you start.

- Making a daily gratitude list.

- Thinking of a reward for when you reach your goal, and make it a great reward.

- Sitting for ideas, to tap into your creative part of your brain.

**Become
a master
of manifestation.**

Mastery

If you have worked through all of the principles up to this point and followed most of the suggestions in each chapter, you are well on your way to making the goal you chose in Prosperity Principle Two a reality.

Once you reach a goal, then repeat the process again, and reach that next goal. Then do it again, and again, and again.

The first five chapters have covered the basics of using the principles to create any goal you set. However, in this chapter, we'll take it to the next level. I call this principle Mastery, because it applies everything you have read so far, and adds to it, so that you become a master of manifestation.

This chapter includes ideas you can use at any time on your journey to riches. I encourage you to begin employing some of them right away.

Master Mind Group

You may have heard of a "Master Mind Group." It's a concept that was introduced by Andrew Carnegie and popularized in Napoleon Hill's writings. The idea is that a group of people, who each have goals, come together to support each other in achieving those goals. This is very effective because Master Mind Groups:

- **Allow you to be around other goal-oriented people.**

- **Help to mine the depths of other smart people.**

- **Give and receive help.**

- **Help you be accountable.**

- **Allow you the opportunity to help others in the group as well.**

☞ DO THIS:
Form a Master Mind Group

Here are some basic rules for forming your own Master Mind Group:

A group should include at least two people, and generally no more than six

Meet consistently, weekly if possible, and in person if possible

Give each member equal time to discuss their goal and their process in making it come true. Make sure that no one uses more time in the group than others.

Allow for constructive ideas and creative problem-solving

Everything said in the group is confidential.

Keep meetings focused only on goals, don't waste time chitchatting about other things.

Disinvite members who don't take the process seriously.

Use this group to help each other—don't just receive help, make sure you help others.

Note—Family members don't usually make great Master Mind Group members as they tend to bring their past ideas about you with them.

☞ DO THIS:
Create Team YOU

Master Mind Groups are great—I've been in many of them over the years. But there is another type of group that can also be beneficial. It's still a group of people, but they have a different focus and it's all about you. That's why I call it Team YOU.

Many people, as they begin a journey of making their goal come true, feel they have to do it all by themselves. The truth is, we don't have to be alone on our goal-making journey. In fact, you will reach your goal even more quickly if you engage with others who can help you. I call this creating Team YOU. Team YOU is a group of people you assemble to support you on your way to achieving your goal. Each member serves a different need you have. Team YOU is your own personal Dream Team.

Here's how you do it:

One a sheet of paper or in your journal, write "Team ME" (or use your name, I called mine "Team JOEL"). Make a list of all the things you need help with. For instance, if you are starting a business but you don't enjoy the accounting and marketing side of things, you might write a list that starts like this:

Accountant
Marketing Expert

Then add all the other people that can help you get your business off the ground: investor, doctor/medical professional, artist, organizer, assistant/intern, etc.

Next, begin filling in the names of the people who can fulfill each role. In the above example, say you don't know any accountants. Then do an internet search to find an accountant, one who can fill the role you have and is in your price range. Don't have a budget (yet)? Then leave it blank, and let other people know you are looking for accounting help. There is even free accounting available (do an internet search) for those who qualify for it. I found some team members on websites like *Fivrr.com*, *Upwork.com*, *Guru.com*, and *Freelancer.com*. These sites are filled with professionals around the world who can help you on a project by project basis for very low fees. (Make sure to explain exactly what you want, get bids, and choose the person carefully.)

Team JOEL has never met all together in person. In fact, there are some people on Team JOEL that I've never met in person, but only communicated with via email and/or phone. But each person on my team is there to help me achieve my goals.

Ask any self-made millionaire: You don't have to do it alone. In fact, it's not only more effective, it's more fun to achieve your goal with the help of others.

Be Teachable

Here's one of those universal truths that you need to ponder:

> ## You don't know what you don't know.

You know?

I've learned that it's important to stay teachable. There are many people who are experts, but the experts that I admire the most probably would not describe themselves as experts. They would probably describe themselves as lifelong learners or students of life. They are always learning and growing and changing, no matter what their age. I've tried to emulate this in my life.

When we believe we are experts, it's harder to be in the mindset to learn new things.

About three years ago, I set a goal to learn Spanish. I hadn't tried to learn a language since I took four years of German in high school (not that I remember any of it). My goal was to have a functional understanding of Spanish in a year. I had no idea how to go about this. I bought a book about learning Spanish and every day I tried to learn a new set of vocabulary words (*el tren, la casa, la pluma*). Then I began learning verbs in the present tense. Pretty soon I found that I needed more information than I could get from just a book. I began watching internet videos and eventually hired a tutor to come to my office once a week on my lunch hour for one-on-one training.

It was a great goal, and it ended up causing several unexpected side effects. First, I fell in love with Spanish-language music, so many different styles! Then I started connecting with Spanish-speaking people in my office and in my church, and they in turn introduced me to authentic Spanish food from their family backgrounds. And then I took my family on trips to various Latin countries and to Spain, where we were able to experience different cultures, each wonderful and enriching.

I thought I was just learning a new language. Three and a half years later, I still work with a tutor and love every minute of it. What I thought was just learning a new skill became an adventure that took me and my family around the world! New friends, new food, new experiences. I've even used my newfound Spanish skills in my business. I didn't know that this one simple decision—to learn Spanish—would change my life so completely. I thought that I just didn't know Spanish, but I didn't know so much more (and I continue to learn!).

Each goal we choose may seem like a just a goal, but when we immerse ourselves in that goal, we are transformed. That doesn't happen unless you have the mindset of being teachable.

Adapt the Principles

So far in this book, you've been exploring the basic Prosperity Principles that self-made millionaires have used to reach their goals. As you move forward, you are going to discover other things that will help you to reach your goals.

In the classes and workshops I've taught over the years, I've seen people reach their goals by taking these ideas and adapting them to their own lives. Here are some of the ways they've done this:

- **Created a Master Mind Group via Zoom or Skype.**

- Created one big goal that they wanted to achieve in a year, and then broke that big goal into twelve smaller goals that lead to the big one, which allowed them to have a monthly goal to reach, and then breaking up the monthly goals into four smaller goals, and then break those up in even smaller goals. At some point this can be obsessive, but if it helps you to achieve goals, then design things as you wish.

- Read an inspirational book each month, to stay motivated and gain new, deeper perspectives. (See Appendix A for a list of books to read either on your own or with others in a monthly inspirational book club.)

- Watched TED and TEDx talks on YouTube.

- Hired a life coach to keep you accountable and challenge you to achieve more.

- Joined an investment club to learn safe ways to invest and increase your money.

This is *your* journey. Make it fun. It's easy to be so focused that we forget to be creative and adaptable.

Your Relationship with Money

One important aspect of making money involves your relationship with money itself. We often block our prosperity with our own negative attitudes about money. Some of these include:

- I'll never be rich.

- I don't deserve riches.

- I'm afraid I'll be forgotten.

- Wanting money is bad.

- Money is dirty.

- I don't know anyone famous or powerful who can help me.

- My parents were terrible with money.

- The system is rigged.

- I've always struggled, and I guess that's my lot in life.

- Something always comes up that seems to require all the money I've saved.

- People always take advantage of me.

- I'll never be paid enough for my job.

- Someday I'll do better, but right now I'll just muddle through.

- I'm the screwup in my family.

☞ DO THIS:
Make Money Your Friend

How do you think about money? Use the following prompts to journal about your thoughts about money, and do so off the top of your head, without overthinking:

I think money is . . .

My parents' relationship with money was . . .

I grew up thinking that money was . . .

My first memory of money is . . .

How did I receive money as a child? And what did I do with it?

When I pay my bills, I feel . . .

On a scale of 1 (least) to 10 (most), my organization with my money and finances is . . .

What scares me about money is . . .

How much money would I need to feel completely safe and comfortable?

Review your answers. How do you feel about what you wrote?

Here's the truth about money: It's neither positive or negative. Money just "is." It's a form of exchange. But we have so many thoughts and emotions around money that can get in our way. **As you continue your journey toward financial mastery, it's important to improve your outlook about money.**

Use the principle of auto-suggestion (from Prosperity Principle Four) to create new ideas about money, and then repeat them over and over. By doing this, you are planting new seeds, or beliefs, that will grow into a whole new relationship with money.

By changing your beliefs from negative to positive, you will have a more positive experience, and make your riches more quickly.

NEGATIVE	POSITIVE
Money is hard to get.	I am a magnet for money.
Money is my enemy.	Money is my friend.
Money is evil.	Money is neutral.
Money belongs to others.	I am worthy of wealth.

The following is a list of words and phrases about money to keep your thoughts about it positive. Use them frequently.

- **Cash**

- **Wealth/wealthy**

- Luxury

- Rich/riches

- Prosperous/prosperity/prosper

- Abundance/abundant

- Affluent

- Well-to-do

- Flush

- Financially independent

- More than enough

- Comfortable

- Upscale

- Upgrade

What other words can you add to this list?

Giving Back

Prosperity Principle Four discussed the Law of Giving and Receiving. Now we are going to take that idea a few steps further. This isn't a life law, but it does create an amazing amount of joy and meaning in your life. It's giving back.

The further we continue on our own journey toward our goal, it's good to take time to shift our focus out of our own life, and the best way to do that is to give to others who can use our help.

There are three main ways we can give to others:

1. Our time
2. Our money
3. Our talents

There is nothing that will make you feel wealthy and fortunate like giving to those who are less fortunate. As little as you may feel you have, you can still find people who can use your time, money, or talents.

When I was at my lowest point financially and carrying a tremendous amount of debt, I was feeling depressed, dark, and overwhelmed by my situation. My own circumstances were all-consuming, and I spent much of each day obsessing over them.

As I began my journey to riches using the principles in this book, I was presented with the opportunity to volunteer for a foundation that was helping people with little or no money and who had chronic illnesses. The person I was assigned to help had his own apartment, but not much else. He was very sick, couldn't walk on his own, and needed a wheelchair to get around. He did have daily caseworkers who came to take care of his medical needs, but he had other needs as well. I was young and didn't quite know how to help him, but I had committed to assisting him one afternoon a week, every week. When I showed up, he would have a list of things he needed me to do—fix things, change lightbulbs, make meals, clean his bedroom or bathroom, do laundry, etc. Eventually the tasks included taking him shopping (which was challenging since I had a tiny car and we needed to take him and his big wheelchair). He would tell me which route to take to each store he wanted me to drive him to.

Over the weeks and months, I learned a lot about this man, discovering that he once held a prominent job and had accomplished many things in his younger life. He wasn't his disease; the disease was something he had. When he died, I was heartbroken. What started like a volunteer job I felt I "should" do ended up being a friendship, and I knew I was privileged to have known him. While I know I was helpful to him, he was invaluable in teaching me about life and death and giving.

What does this have to do with your million-dollar journey? Nothing and everything. What I want you to know is that

by giving to others, you become richer in very deep ways.

I encourage you to find an established organization that you can volunteer for. Perhaps it's with people who have illnesses, like I did. Or maybe you can volunteer to give your time by mentoring young underprivileged kids who need help learning how to interview for jobs. Or at a women's shelter. Or for your local cat or dog shelter. Or short-term fostering kids in need. Or delivering food to the elderly. Or . . . there are countless ways to volunteer your time, your money, and your talents.

☞ DO THIS:
Give Back

Think about giving back. How can you give back? What's the first thing that pops into your head? Write it below:

_____

_____

Consider doing some online research and finding a place that might be thrilled to have what you are able to give. If I were a betting man, I would bet that you will feel like what you gained was worth . . . millions.

Prosperity and Forgiveness

If you want the real secret to creating more prosperity in your life, it's not a stock tip or a lottery ticket. It's forgiveness.

I don't think there is a scientific study that shows the exact correlation between doing forgiveness work and riches, but I have plenty of anecdotal evidence. I first came across this theory over thirty years ago in a seminar on creating more wealth consciousness. The speaker—I can't even remember who it was now, but I remember his message—said that **we tend to have more focus and inner mental capacity for success when we clear up the things in our consciousness that clutter it.**

That made sense to me—it's easy to be distracted by things that don't necessarily help me or create more positivity. It's like a computer that is slowed down by too many programs that are running in the background. If you want the computer to run faster, then you close those programs, and even better, you delete unnecessary programs altogether.

That's what forgiveness does. It clears out unwanted programs that are running in your head and slowing things down. It does something else as well—it makes life better and happier. After all, what good are riches and reaching goals if you aren't happy?

In case you're not exactly clear on what I mean by forgiveness, I've compiled some descriptions below:

FORGIVENESS ISN'T	FORGIVENESS IS
condoning bad behavior or people	coming to peace about difficult situations
letting people "off the hook"	letting yourself off the hook
a onetime event	a process
to free other people	to free yourself
always easy	worth it
sweeping something under the rug	feeling your feelings and honoring them
dependent on the other person	for yourself, regardless of the other person
easy to hold on to	a way to let go of what weighs you down
turning the other cheek	creating boundaries
rehashing the past	letting go so you can move forward
weakness	recognizing your strength

I began the book by talking about the inner work necessary to create an attitude and a capability to create more wealth in your life. Forgiveness is like the honors course version of inner work. If you aren't convinced, then move to the next section. But if you are intrigued and want to experience the benefits of forgiveness, a simple method follows below.

☞ DO THIS:
Forgive Someone

There are many different ways you can forgive others and live a freer life. Here is one way that can help, a beginner's guide to forgiving. If this starts a journey for you, then I encourage you to explore it in more depth. This exercise may help you forgive others easily and quickly, or it may begin the process of forgiving certain people, which could take time and patience. Note that this is meant to be a basic forgiveness exercise. If at any time it is too overwhelming, that's the sign that something deeper might be happening, and it's important to take that seriously. If that's the case, stop this exercise and seek out a counselor or licensed professional to help support you through your process.

Close your eyes, and take a few deep, cleansing breaths.
Think of one person who hurt you, picture them in your mind.

In your mind, tell them how they hurt you and how it made you feel.

Be thorough, be honest.

Ask yourself, "Is it possible for me to forgive this person?"

Then ask, "Will I ever forgive this person?"

Then ask, "When will I forgive this person?"

Then ask, "How does not forgiving this person impact my life?"

Then ask, "Am I ready to begin forgiving this person?"

If not, then take a breath, and honor the fact that you started the process. Repeat later.

If yes, then take a breath, and tell the person you forgive them. You can use any words you want.

Now take a breath, release this experience, and open your eyes.

Record any thoughts you want to remember in your journal.

Repeat this exercise as often as you want. Remember, forgiveness is a process and it may take several times before you're able to forgive certain people or experiences. Respect your feelings.

Forgiveness is meant to release emotional baggage so you can travel through your life more lightly. There are many different ways to forgive; I encourage you to do some more research on other ways if the above method doesn't work for you.

Stop:

- Thinking you are limited in your opportunities and potential.

- Believing you have to do your journey by yourself, or that you're all alone.

- Playing small and weak.

- Holding on to resentments or anger.

Start:

- Surrounding yourself with like-minded people who support you.

- Surprising yourself by how far you can go and how much you can do.

- Forgiving others and releasing any negativity.

- Living your life like the prosperous person you are!

AFTERWORD

Beyond Millions

Thank you for reading this book. My hope is that the Prosperity Principles have helped you begin your journey toward reaching your financial goals—and any goals you might have for your life.

Here's something I learned along the way that surprised me. My first big goal was to become debt-free, and I achieved that in three and a half years (versus the twenty-eight years I was told it would take). Then I set a goal to save a certain amount of money in my savings account, and I achieved that far more quickly than I would have guessed. Then I made another monetary goal and reached it. And then another monetary goal and reached it. And another, and another, and then . . . well, the truth is I got dissatisfied with goals that were only financial in nature.

If you had told me when I was nearly $60,000 in debt that I would eventually have enough money and be doing so well that reaching monetary goals would begin to lose their meaning, I'm not sure I would have believed it. Remember that with goals, I like to attach a meaning to them, which gives them extra "charge."

Please understand that I was (and am) grateful for all of the monetary goals that I made and reached. But after a while I needed to find new goals, ones that fulfilled other needs or desires in my life. So my goals evolved as I evolved. That's when I discovered that the principles in this book work for anything you desire.

Let me repeat something I wrote at the beginning of this book:

For me, getting out of financial peril and into financial abundance was paramount. My financial situation was so difficult that nearly everything else took a back seat to it. I thought about it every day, because every day I either had to find ways to pay bills or worry about how I was going to pay my rent and buy food. So when I discovered these Prosperity Principles (in all their various forms), it felt like the universe had thrown me a lifeline.

I used the Prosperity Principles and my situation changed from dangerous to barely making it, to uncomfortable but okay, to having just a little more than nothing, to having a little extra, to having quite a bit extra, to living in comfort, and beyond. When I started this journey, I was in a financial emergency, so my goals were all financial. Eventually, though, once I moved into a place where my finances were growing and I felt good, I wanted to use the Prosperity Principles in other ways, for other things. And not just "things" but for experiences and qualities as well: travel, adventure, creative outlets, love, health, peace, joy, and more.

My greatest hope for you is that you use the Prosperity Principles for whatever it is you most desire in your life. If you have financial needs, then use them to reach your financial goals. Use the Prosperity Principles for anything else you want as well. They are principles for life, a creative formula to use as you wish. We are all 100 percent responsible for our own lives, so what you do and how you live matters. You are important. Positive action creates positive results. May your future be prosperous!

APPENDIX A

University of Success

Below is a selection of some of the greatest prosperity books ever written. I encourage you to read from them daily, to continue to be inspired and expanded in your thoughts and actions.

You can also form a Prosperity Book Club—with your Master Mind Group members, your success partner, or any small group of people who are dedicated to growing their prosperity consciousness. These books are perfect for study and discussion.

The Encyclopedia of Wealth compiled by Chris Gentry (Hampton Roads). This incredible volume contains twelve classic books, including some on this list.

Think and Grow Rich by Napoleon Hill (St. Martin's Essentials)

As a Man Thinketh by James Allen (St. Martin's Essentials)

The Science of Getting Rich by Wallace Wattles (St. Martin's Essentials)

The Power of Your Subconscious Mind by Joseph Murphy (St. Martin's Essentials)

Success Habits by Napoleon Hill (St. Martin's Essentials)

Spiritual Economics by Eric Butterworth (Unity Books)

How to Live on 24 Hours a Day by Harold Bennett (St. Martin's Essentials)

The Million Dollar Secret Hidden In Your Mind by Anthony Norvell (TarcherPerigee)

The Complete Game of Life by Florence Scovel Shinn (Hampton Roads)

The Conquest of Poverty by Helen Wilmans (various editions available)

The Ideal Made Real by Christian Larson (various editions available)

It Works by RHJ (DeVorss)

The Greatest Miracle in the World by Og Mandino (Bantam)

How to Win Friends and Influence People by Dale Carnegie (Simon & Schuster)

The Magic of Thinking Big by David J. Schwarz (Touchstone)

Psycho-cybernetics by Maxwell Maltz (TarcherPerigee)

Acres of Diamonds by Russell H. Conwell (various editions available)

A Message to Garcia by Elbert Hubbard (various editions available)

You2 (You Squared) by Price Pritchett (from the author)

Money Is My Friend by Phil Laut (Ballantine)

The Abundance Book by John Randolph Price (Hay House)

Silva Mind Control by Jose Silva (Simon & Schuster)

Three Little Words by U.S. Andersen (Wilshire)

Success Quotes

Let these twenty quotes on prosperity inspire you. If there are any that you particularly like, write them out on a sticky note and place where you can see them often. Don't stop with these quotes; find as many quotes that inspire you and keep them handy to read when you need them most.

—◆—

"I know the price of success: dedication, hard work and an unremitting devotion to the things you want to see happen."

—*Frank Lloyd Wright*

—◆—

"I have learned that success is to be measured not so much by the position that one has reached in life as by the obstacles which he has had to overcome while trying to succeed."

—*Booker T. Washington*

⸺◈⸺

"When I chased after money, I never had enough. When I got my life on purpose and focused on giving of myself and everything that arrived into my life, then I was prosperous."

—*Wayne Dyer*

⸺◈⸺

"Action is the foundational key to all success."

—*Pablo Picasso*

⸺◈⸺

"The most common way people give up their power
is by thinking they don't have any."
– *Alice Walker*

—◆—

"Prosperity is a way of living and thinking, and not
just money or things. Poverty is a way of living and
thinking, and not just a lack of money or things."
—*Eric Butterworth*

—◆—

"What's money? A man is a success if he gets up
in the morning and goes to bed at night and in
between does what he wants to do."
—*Bob Dylan*

—◆—

"Without continual growth and progress, such words as improvement, achievement, and success have no meaning."

—*Benjamin Franklin*

—◊—

"I attribute my success to this—I never gave or took any excuse."

—*Florence Nightingale*

—◊—

"Success isn't about the end result, it's about what you learn along the way."

—*Vera Wang*

—◊—

"I planned my success.
I knew it was going to happen."

—*Erykah Badu*

———◇———

"Live as if you were to die tomorrow. Learn as if
you were to live forever."

—*Mahatma Gandhi*

———◇———

"The difference between a successful person
and others is not a lack of strength, not a lack of
knowledge, but rather a lack of will."

—*Vince Lombardi*

———◇———

"It is our choices, that show what we truly are,
far more than our abilities."

—*J. K. Rowling*

———◇◆◇———

"Every great dream begins with a dreamer. Always
remember, you have within you the strength, the
patience, and the passion to reach for the stars
to change the world."

—*Harriet Tubman*

———◇◆◇———

"Take up one idea. Make that one idea your life –
think of it, dream of it, live on that idea. Let the
brain, muscles, nerves, every part of your body, be
full of that idea, and just leave every other idea alone.
This is the way to success."

—*Swami Vivekananda*

———◇◆◇———

"Develop success from failures.
Discouragement and failure are two of the surest
stepping stones to success."
—*Dale Carnegie*

"If you don't design your own life plan,
chances are you'll fall into someone else's plan.
And guess what they have planned for you?
Not much."
—*Jim Rohn*

———◇———

"If you want to make a permanent change, stop
focusing on the size of your problems and start
focusing on the size of you!"
—*T. Harv Eker*

———◇———

"You don't become what you want,
you become what you believe."

—*Oprah Winfrey*

APPENDIX C

List of Exercises

Here's a list of all the exercises included throughout the book for quick reference. You'll want to practice some of them again (and again). They can help you reassess your goals, evaluate your progress, and give you forward momentum as you travel your path to prosperity.

About the Author

Joel Fotinos is the vice president and editorial director at St. Martin's Press and the author of several books, including *The Think and Grow Rich Workbook*. Fotinos has been featured in many magazines and newspapers, and was given *Science of Mind* magazine's first Spiritual Hero of the Year award. A licensed minister with the Centers for Spiritual Living, Fotinos travels the country giving talks and workshops on spirituality and inspiration. He lives in New Jersey.

Hampton Roads Publishing Company

. . . for the evolving human spirit

Hampton Roads Publishing Company publishes books on a variety of subjects, including spirituality, health, and other related topics.

For a copy of our latest trade catalog, call (978) 465-0504 or visit our distributor's website at *www.redwheelweiser.com*. You can also sign up for our newsletter and special offers by going to *www.redwheelweiser.com/newsletter/*.